John Gross was Editor of the *Times Literary Supplement* from 1974–81. Educated at City of London School and Wadham College, Oxford, he had a brief period in publishing before he was appointed Assistant Lecturer in English at Queen Mary College, London, in 1957. In 1962 he was elected Fellow of King's College, Cambridge, a position that he held until 1965. Subsequently he was Literary Editor of *New Statesman*. In 1969 he was awarded the Duff Cooper Memorial Prize for his study, *The Rise and Fall of the Man of Letters* (1969).

Modern Masters

Joyce

John Gross

Fontana/Collins

First published in Fontana 1971
Third Impression, with corrections, October 1976
Fifth Impression September 1982
Copyright © John Gross 1971

Made and printed in Great Britain by
William Collins Sons & Co. Ltd, Glasgow

Contents

1 Modern Instances

By the time James Joyce came to write *Finnegans Wake*, with its cycloramic view of world history, he may well have felt that such categories as 'modern' or 'traditional' no longer made much sense when applied to his work; but for his early admirers he was above all else a Modern, intoxicatingly so. T. S. Eliot, in 1922, talked of him as the man who had 'killed the nineteenth century'. For Edmund Wilson, in *Axel's Castle* (1931), he was 'the great poet of a new phase of the human consciousness'. And however much recent critics may wrangle over the exact course of literary Modernism, the publication of *Ulysses* remains one of the few landmarks on which everybody can still agree.

Up to a point the force of Joyce's original impact can be accounted for purely in terms of his technical daring. Overturning the orderly assumptions of most previous fiction, experimenting with hybrid styles and abrupt transitions, he opened up possibilities which other writers have been exploring ever since. But a major artist is more than the sum of his techniques, and behind remarks such as those of Eliot and Wilson there also lurk large extra-literary considerations. In Eliot's case, *Ulysses* signalled the final collapse (hastened, no doubt, by the First World War) of a social order with which the artist could in any meaningful way identify. Where the classic nineteenth-century novel, however critical of social evils, presupposed at least the distant hope of redemption, the only real future for fiction now lay in detached irony and the long perspective of myth. Wilson, on the other hand, was more concerned with Joyce as (among other things) the literary equivalent of a modern scientist, constantly shifting his angle of vision, breaking down the 'continuum' of behaviour into a series of tiny discrete 'events'. Other critics in the twenties and thirties, as they groped around for illuminating comparisons, hit on cubism, psychoanalysis, the cinema, even jazz. Wyndham Lewis, bundling Joyce together with philosophers like Bergson and Whitehead, castigated him for his typically twentieth-century obsession with Time; the Hungarian artist Moholy-Nagy applauded him as a writer of the Machine Age, who had learned how to streamline language and handle words like an industrial technologist.

Some of these analogies now look badly dated. Others are still genuinely useful in helping to relate Joyce, however loosely, to the intellectual climate of the age in which he wrote, and at least one of them, the comparison with Einsteinian physics, has Joyce's own blessing.[1] But it is important to remember that they *are* only analogies. As imaginative literature, his work is an end in itself, and his ideas are of very little interest except in so far as they contribute to that end. This is certainly not to say that he can't be intellectually stimulating as well as moving or entertaining. No English-language writer, for example, fits in better with the notion that Western culture in the present century has been marked by a profound 'language revolution', a new awareness of the extent to which the world we live in is a linguistic product. But it is his practice, not his theorising (if one can call it that) which is significant in this respect. His experiments with word-formation and syn-

1. The most direct acknowledgement can be found at the beginning of the fable of the Mookse and the Gripes: 'Eins within a space ...' i.e. once upon a space-time. For Joyce's attempts to reproduce relativity and the uncertainty principle in the *Wake*, see Clive Hart, *Structure and Motif in Finnegans Wake* (1962), pp. 64–6.

tax don't make him a linguist; they simply provide some
unusually rich data for the linguists to get to work on.

Much the same is true of Joyce and psychoanalysis,
although here the situation is complicated by the fact
that he was generally hostile to both Freud and Jung, and
had some unsatisfactory personal dealings with the latter
('the Swiss Tweedledum, who is not to be confused with
the Viennese Tweedledee'). His hostility did not preclude
a certain intellectual indebtedness, and in some ways the
Wake can be seen as a prolonged and defiant attempt at
self-analysis—'I can psoakoonaloose myself any time I
want . . .' But much more to the point are the pressures
which compelled him to use all his books as outlets for
his emotional conflicts, and the literary ethos which encouraged him to dramatise them in such intimate detail.
Once again, what he provides is the raw material : how
we interpret it will depend on our own presuppositions.
The *Wake*, for instance, has sometimes been taken as
exemplifying the Collective Unconscious, 'the law of the
jungerl', but personally I have no doubt that it is the
Viennese Tweedledee whose insights are again and
again confirmed by Earwicker, and by Bloom and
Stephen Dedalus as well.

Something of this will, I hope, emerge in the following
pages. On the other hand the reader will find virtually no
mention of the innovation which originally earned
Ulysses its most widespread notoriety, its sexual and
scatological frankness. Nor, I imagine, will he expect to :
at this hour in the day there is nothing new to be said on
such a topic, and by comparison with what we have
come to take for granted in recent years Joyce's 'out-
spokeness' now looks rather tame. As a shock-tactic it
belongs to a moment which has passed, and which can
never be repeated. Yet we should not lose sight of how
much it meant to him (and to his serious readers) at the
time, how essential a part of his enterprise it was to drag

forbidden material into the daylight. By breaking the most jealously-guarded of literary taboos, he gave notice that the entire range of experience was grist to his epic: the man who was prepared to use four-letter words in print would stop at nothing, or so it seemed in 1922.

Finally, it is worth bearing in mind, when talking about Joyce's modernism, that in some ways the modernistic label looks incongruous on him. At times he seems more like a man who has just clambered out of the Middle Ages, with his odd mixture of humanism and superstition, crabbed scholasticism and Rabelaisian exuberance. More immediately, his outlook was formed before 1914 (and his masterpiece is set in 1904): in his tacit political assumptions he belonged to an age which had never experienced totalitarianism or total war. And yet there is also a sense in which, like any classic, he transcends his period, and confronts us—in *Ulysses*, at least—with the perennial facts of human nature. Every great writer was once a Modern Master, but the final proof of his mastery is that it should outlive his modernity.

2   The Haunted Inkbottle

I

James Augustine Joyce was born in Dublin in 1882, the eldest of the ten children of John Stanislaus Joyce and his wife Mary Jane ('May'). At the time of his birth, and for some years afterwards, his father had a job in the office of the Collector of Rates. Educated at Clongowes Wood College, a leading Catholic boarding-school, and then, after a short break, at Belvedere College, a Catholic day school in Dublin, Joyce entered University College, Dublin, in 1898, and graduated with a degree in modern languages four years later. By this time he had already begun to make his mark as a literary controversialist; he had also committed to his notebooks dozens of poems and prose sketches, or 'epiphanies'. Subsequently he left Dublin for Paris in order to study medicine, but returned home the following year on account of his mother's fatal illness. He taught for a brief period in a private school, published a handful of stories and poems, and won a bronze medal for singing in the national music festival. In June 1904 he met and fell in love with Nora Barnacle, a twenty-year-old girl from Galway who was working as a chambermaid at Finn's Hotel. They left for the Continent in the October of that year and set up house in Pola, on the Adriatic, where Joyce had been offered a teaching-post at the local Berlitz school. The following spring they moved on to Trieste, where Joyce again took up a post as a Berlitz teacher. Apart from a short unhappy spell in Rome, where Joyce worked in a bank, this was to be their home for the next ten years. Their two children, Giorgio and Lucia, were both born there; they were also joined after a few months by Joyce's brother Stanislaus, the one member of his family with whom he remained on close terms.

Before leaving Ireland Joyce had started work on an autobiographical novel, *Stephen Hero*, which he eventually abandoned, and on a collection of short stories, *Dubliners*, which he completed and submitted to a publisher in 1905. It was not until 1914 that the book finally appeared, however, after a series of angry disputes, the worst of them taking place in 1912 on the occasion of what was to prove Joyce's last visit to Dublin. (On a previous visit, in 1909, he had been badly shaken by the malicious allegations of an old acquaintance who claimed, quite falsely, that he had shared Nora's favours.) Meanwhile he brought out a volume of poems, *Chamber Music*, and recast the story of Stephen Hero as *A Portrait of the Artist as a Young Man*, which was serialised in an English little magazine, the *Egoist*, in 1914–15. In the course of 1914 he also wrote most of his one surviving play, *Exiles*, and began mapping out *Ulysses*.

On account of difficulties created by the First World War—Trieste was at that time part of the Austro-Hungarian Empire—the Joyces moved to Zurich in 1915. With the publication of the *Portrait* in book-form Joyce began to acquire a small but distinguished following in England and America, and interest grew as excerpts from *Ulysses* appeared in the *Egoist* and the *Little Review* (New York). At the same time his financial situation was gradually alleviated by outside help : in the first instance, minor grants from the Royal Literary Fund and the Civil List, procured chiefly by Pound and Yeats, then much larger sums given to him by an anonymous admirer—as it transpired, Harriet Shaw Weaver, editor of the *Egoist*—and by Mrs Edith Rockefeller McCormick.

(Miss Weaver, the daughter of a country doctor from Cheshire, was to remain his most loyal and generous patron.) The Zurich years were also notable for Joyce's brief romantic infatuation with a young Swiss girl, Martha Fleischmann, and for his prolonged wrangle with the British Consulate General, a grotesque storm in a teacup which had its origins in a quarrel over the cost of a pair of trousers used in a local production of *The Importance of Being Earnest*.

Joyce left Switzerland and returned to Trieste in 1919, but in the summer of 1920, urged on by Pound, he decided to settle in Paris. Later that year the *Little Review* was forced to suspend its serialisation of *Ulysses*, following a complaint lodged by the New York Society for the Prevention of Vice. It was becoming clear that the book, now nearing completion, had no chance of finding a publisher in England or America, and Joyce readily agreed to the suggestion of Sylvia Beach, an American expatriate living in Paris, that she should publish it under the imprint of the bookshop which she owned, Shakespeare and Company. After a frantc last-minute race against time, finished copies were finally placed in his hands on February 2nd, 1922, his fortieth birthday.

The furore over *Ulysses* made him one of the most celebrated literary figures of the day. To the general public he was the man who had written a dirty book; a famous *New Yorker* cartoon of the period showed an American matron hesitantly asking a Parisian shop-assistant, 'Avez-vous *Ulysses*?', and there was a brisk bootleg trade in the book, to say nothing of a pirated American version, until Judge Woolscy's ruling that it was not a pornographic work enabled a New York publishing house to bring out an authorised edition in 1934. (The first English edition followed two years later.) To the avant-garde, on the other hand, Joyce was a hero, a saint of literature. Young writers paid their respects to him, and disciples hung on his words. But even the warmest admirers of *Ulysses* tended to be disconcerted by the first published fragments of the new book which he had begun writing in 1923, under the provisional title of *Work in Progress*. Joyce felt this lack of support keenly, especially coming at a time when he was threatened with the possibility of blindness; the long series of ophthalmic operations to which he submitted in the twenties led him to speak of himself as 'an international eyesore'. The thirties were overshadowed for him by an even heavier burden, the worsening mental condition of Lucia, who suffered a severe breakdown in 1932. (It seems to have been partly precipitated by the marriage ceremony which her parents had gone through the previous year.) For a long time Joyce refused to admit that there was anything basically wrong with her, but her behaviour grew steadily more erratic, and finally, in 1936, she had to be committed to a *maison de santé*.

Despite these tribulations, Joyce pressed ahead with *Work in Progress*. A number of sections were published in book-form; others appeared in various periodicals, notably the Paris review *transition*, which was run by his ardent admirers Eugene and Maria Jolas. (It was Eugene Jolas who first succeeded in solving the riddle which he enjoyed setting his friends and guessing that the book was ultimately to be called *Finnegans Wake*.) Under Joyce's supervision a group of disciples, including Samuel Beckett, also published a defence of the whole undertaking, *Our Exagmination round his Factification for Incamination of Work in Progress* (1929). Between them, his labours on the book and his private troubles were now absorbing almost all his energies, although he did allow himself one major distraction in the early thirties : a campaign on behalf of John Sullivan, an Irish operatic tenor whom he believed had been the victim of unfair treatment by the opera authorities.

Finnegans Wake was completed in 1938 and published in 1939. Disheartened by its generally hostile or uncomprehending reception, Joyce lingered on in Paris after the outbreak of war, but in Christmas 1939 he settled in the village of St Gérand-le-Puy, near Vichy. After almost exactly a year he was forced to move on again, this time to Zurich. He died four weeks after his arrival there, on January 13th, 1941, following an operation for a perforated ulcer. Nora, who continued to make her home in Zurich, died in 1951.

Those are the bare bones of the story. If Joyce were an abstract thinker, or a scientist, or even another kind of writer, they might suffice. But as it is, he is an artist whose ideas and attitudes only hang together in the context of his own experience, and before trying to assess his books we must look a little more closely at the personality they reveal.

II

In the remarkable letter which he sent to Ibsen at the age of nineteen, Joyce reserved his warmest praise for the dramatist's 'lofty impersonal power'. He was proclaiming an ideal as well as paying homage, and at first sight it is tempting to describe his own achievement in similar terms. One need only think of the level tones and the deadpan manner of *Dubliners*; or of Stephen Dedalus's account of the godlike artist, hidden behind his handiwork, refining his personality out of existence; or of how far Joyce had put the raw self-justification of *Stephen Hero* behind him when he came to write the *Portrait of the Artist*, where much the same autobiographical material is shaped, edited, tinged with irony, set at a distance. As for *Ulysses*, it is at the very least the epic of a city (some would say of the modern world), with a commonplace man-in-the-street hero and the weight of an entire culture behind it. And the 'monomyth' of *Finnegans Wake* goes further still: its hero is, so to speak, even more of an Everyman, and it aspires to bring nothing less than the whole of history within its grasp.

Small wonder, then, that the legend of a cold, inscrutable, clinically detached Joyce first took root. It was reinforced by rumours of his aloofness and elusiveness as a man, while the literary climate in which he worked did little to discourage it: a year or two before *Ulysses* appeared, T. S. Eliot had set the course for a generation and more of anti-biographical criticism in 'Tradition and the Individual Talent', with his account of the artist's progress as 'a continual extinction of personality', and his emphasis on the gap between 'the man who suffers and the mind which creates'. Joyce's later books are so intricate, moreover, that there is a natural tendency for the reader who falls under their spell to submit to them on their own terms, to concentrate on deciphering them without questioning their basic assumptions. From here it is only a short step to treating Joyce as virtually superhuman, a fabulous artificer who had every conceivable move worked out in advance.

With the years, however, the tradition of Joyce's impersonality has become harder and harder to sustain. On the contrary, it is now clear that few writers, in Stanislaus Joyce's words, 'have ever exploited the minute, unpromising material of their experience so thoroughly', that he was indeed the 'egoarch' which he accuses himself of being in *Finnegans Wake*. (In one of his letters, incidentally, he applies the same term to Ibsen, lofty impersonal power notwithstanding.) The monumental researches of his biographer, Richard Ellmann, the publication of his letters, the gradual uncovering of hidden references and motifs by a small army of Joycean scholars have all helped to build up the picture of a man

whose intimate presence can be felt in almost every line
he wrote. We may still maintain, if we choose, that
Joyce is impersonal in the sense that any true artist is by
definition, in the sense that a work of art and an autobiography belong to different orders of being; but we
ought to recognise at the same time how central a significance Joyce himself attributed to the autobiographical
element in literature. In the end it seems plain that
Stephen Dedalus's disquisition on Shakespeare in the
library scene in *Ulysses*, however much it may be under-
cut by the author's irony, is meant to be taken fairly
seriously. For Stephen, Shakespeare's personal history
looms up everywhere in his work. The ghost and the
prince, Iago and the Moor, tight-fisted Shylock and 'pros-
perous Prospero' all embody aspects of their creator—
and one can claim as much, with a good deal more cer-
tainty, of Leopold Bloom, to say nothing of Stephen himself.

It isn't just a question of identifying prototypes and
tracking down personal allusions. Many of these turn
out to be trivial; others are best forgotten. In the 'Lotus-
Eaters' episode, for example, when Bloom sees a young
boy hanging around outside a pub waiting for his 'da'
and smoking 'a chewed fagbutt', he checks his impulse to
'tell him if he smokes he won't grow' and thinks to himself : 'O let him ! His life isn't such a bed of roses !' Quite
apart from contributing unobtrusively to the flower-
strewn imagery of 'The Lotus-Eaters', the sentence is
beautifully in character; solicitous, tolerant, at once a
cliché and more than a cliché. It then positively detracts
from one's pleasure to be told that Joyce was also working in a private reference to a girl student of his in
Trieste who used to smoke cigarettes made out of rose-
leaves. There are a number of occasions, on the other
hand, where a passage is virtually pointless without
some knowledge of the corresponding biographical

event. For the purist, this is indefensible; less exacting
readers have to turn to the commentators for help, or
resign themselves to remaining in the dark. Either way,
however, these local conundrums are only of limited
importance. Where a knowledge of Joyce's life really
counts, where it can modify a reader's fundamental response to his work, is in bringing out the full egocentric
and conflict-ridden nature of his genius. Seen in this light,
his books derive their power from the intensity of his
obsessions and the energy with which he tried to master
them. They are acts of concealment and exposure, of
revenge and reconciliation, of self-purgation and self-
definition.

His neurotic disposition manifests itself in many ways,
most strikingly, perhaps, in his sense of being a preordained victim, his dark talk of betrayal, his brooding
preoccupation—seen at its creepiest in *Exiles*—with the
possibility of being cuckolded. He was also prey to
vague feelings of anxiety and inadequacy (alternating
with moods of self-insulating arrogance); while, more
specifically, his books and his letters to Nora both reveal
a cluster of classic Krafft–Ebbing symptoms—fear of
homosexuality, underwear-fetishism, masochistic and
voyeuristic fantasies, the 'cloacal obsession' which H. G.
Wells detected as long ago as 1917 in his review of the
Portrait of the Artist. Nor is it a question of prying; in his
later work Joyce brings this kind of material insistently
to the fore. In the index to the *Reader's Guide to Finnegans Wake* the author is reduced to writing *passim* next
to the entries under Defecation and Urination, and he
might well have done the same for Perversion. The
Wake fairly bristles with surrealist scatology; it would
have had even more trouble than *Ulysses* getting past the
censors when it first appeared if its full implications had
been spelt out in plain English.

Of all Joyce's emotions, as they figure in his work, the

strongest were undoubtedly those centring on his father. In the earlier books they tend to be predominantly negative, not without good reason. From most points of view John Joyce was a highly unsatisfactory parent: selfish, irresponsible, a heavy drinker, 'a praiser of his own past'. In the years when his eldest son was growing up, his fortunes (like those of John Shakespeare and John Dickens) were on the downward slide, and poverty only served to embitter him and increase his ill-treatment of wife and children. It is true that James was his favourite —even when the family were short of food he gave him money to buy foreign books; but he inevitably came to personify the seamy side of Dublin, the little world of half-maudlin, half-malicious ne'er-do-wells which has its most unflattering memorial in *Dubliners*. And behind the resentment which his actual behaviour inspired on Joyce's part, one can sense a more primitive and irrational hostility. In one of his earliest essays Joyce quotes with evident approval from the savage childhood recollections of the nineteenth-century Irish poet Mangan— 'my father was a boa-constrictor'—and adds that 'they who think such a terrible tale is a figment of a disordered brain do not know how keenly a sensitive boy suffers from contact with a gross nature'. The father is coarse, menacing, liable to crush the son to death. By being made to appear in the *Portrait* and *Ulysses* under the name of Simon Dedalus he is also associated, as several critics have pointed out, with the sin of simony—literally, the buying and selling of ecclesiastical preferments, metaphorically, the corruption and decay which the young Joyce saw as characteristic of the world into which he had been born. A further function of the name, it has been plausibly suggested, is to provide a link with Simon Moonan, the schoolboy in the *Portrait* who is flogged for an obscure 'unnatural' misdemeanour. Moonan is an older boy's 'suck'—a queer, ugly word, Stephen thinks, reminding him of the occasion in a hotel washroom when he listened to the sound of dirty water going down a plug-hole after his father had pulled out the stopper.

Yet although Simon Dedalus is viewed without affection in the *Portrait*, at the outset of the book there are just the glimmerings of a different attitude. The opening paragraphs form a compact, highly charged overture, rather ominous in its effect, with the father quickly established as an alien physical presence: he has a hairy face, he doesn't smell as nice as the child's mother. But in the very first sentence of all he appears in a sympathetic light: 'Once upon a time and a very good time it was ...' He is telling a story, furnishing the infant Stephen with a model of the art which he is one day to practise. It would of course be an over-simplification to say that as an artist Joyce was his father's son. Whatever he inherited, he added to and immeasurably transformed. But what can, I think, fairly be claimed is that his major achievements, and the spirit of comedy in which they were conceived, only became possible once he began to acknowledge the affection which he felt for his father, and the debt which he owed him. To acknowledge them in writing, that is; in real life (unlike most of the other Joyce children) he had never made any secret of his admiration. Along with his faults, John Joyce was a man of considerable accomplishments: a gifted singer, a mimic, a raconteur, a seasoned Dublin character with an explosive turn of phrase and an outstanding talent for vituperation. Most of these attributes, notably his humour and his love of music, were transmitted direct to his favourite son. There is little of the lonely *Sturm und Drang* hero about the Joyce of student days who can be glimpsed in the memoirs of contemporaries such as Padraic Colum and Judge Sheehy, taking part in amateur theatricals or singing comic and sentimental ballads from his father's repertoire. But the expansive side of Joyce's nature clashed with his youthful image of himself as a romantic artist and with his desperate need to assert his independence; it was only gradually that he saw his way to incorporating it into his art.

Ulysses and *Finnegans Wake* both represent a turning back towards his father's world. At first sight it may seem perverse to make this claim for *Ulysses*, the book in which Simon Dedalus is pushed to the sidelines and finally discarded in favour of Bloom, a father-substitute who is his moral superior and in many ways his complete antithesis. (Only for one brief moment, while Bloom listens to Simon singing the lament from *Martha* in the bar of the Ormond hotel, are they fused together as 'Siopold'.) But the book celebrates the vitality of much that it formally deplores, and Joyce himself can be called on to testify how far his father's spirit pervades its pages: 'The humour of *Ulysses* is his; its people are his friends. The book is his spittin' image.' Finally, in *Finnegans Wake* father and son 'reamalgamerge' as H. C. Earwicker. Not entirely : they still have their fierce and even potentially murderous clashes, most notably when Buckley shoots the Russian General. But the violence is contained and absorbed by the larger dream-framework, while it is the two warring brothers who are meant to embody the principle of eternal conflict in the *Wake* (and self-dramatising, self-exiled Shem is mocked at for having boasted that his father was a 'boer constructor'). As for the sexual stresses of the father-and-son relationship, Joyce's ability to confront fantasies which would once have frightened him can be gauged from a passage such as the tranquil, almost pastoral description of the paternal buttocks in terms of the geography of Phoenix Park. This relative equanimity is achieved by treating Earwicker simultaneously as a god and as a man with a guilty secret. The sense of guilt can never be abolished, but it can be alleviated by being shared – universalised, in fact, so that the Creator himself becomes a sinner. In the words of one of the most persuasive interpreters of the *Wake*, J. S. Atherton, Joyce 'saw God as a figure very like his own father: erring, irascible, lovable; and in *Finnegans Wake* he amuses himself by creating a mock theology in which his father is enthroned as God'.

Father and fatherland count for so much in Joyce's work that at first one can easily underestimate the strength of his attachment to his mother. In the *Portrait* Mrs Dedalus is a shadowy figure; in *Ulysses* she is already dead, a reproachful ghost. It would be hard to gather from either book, for instance, that May Joyce was almost as devoted to music as her husband. But there are hints (and in the case of *Stephen Hero* rather more than hints) of the extent to which Joyce remained anxious for her approval, even while breaking away from her and even in matters which he knew lay beyond her intellectual grasp. Not that he had any real reason to doubt her love. She appears to have been an admirable mother; her few surviving letters (written to Joyce during his early visits to Paris) reveal her as selfless, longsuffering, protective without being possessive. In her son's mind she naturally came to be associated with images of tenderness and warmth. But his feelings about her were also distorted by the neurotic misgivings which were later to characterise his attitude to women in general: even the cuckoldry obsession surely had its origins in the bewilderment of the baby boy realising for the first time that there was another man in his mother's life. Thirsting for reassurance, yet at the same time resentful of the hold which she had over him, he was led to test her affection by wounding her where it hurt most, by ostentatiously spurning her simple Catholic piety. Fantasy exaggerated the offence: Stephen Dedalus refuses his dying mother's request to kneel and pray at her bedside, although in reality it was an uncle whose peremptory order Joyce disobeyed after his mother had already sunk into a coma. And the remorse which runs through *Ulysses* is correspondingly bitter, coming to its climax in the wonderful scene in 'Circe' (which only an over-refined taste would find too theatrical) where the mother rises from the grave: 'All must go through it, Stephen ... Years and years I loved you, O my son, my first-born, when you lay in my womb.'

To some extent Joyce tended to think of Ireland itself as an oppressed and oppressive mother; equally, in more exalted moments he was capable of identifying the essential spirit of the country with Nora, especially with Nora in her quasimaternal role:

> O take me into your soul of souls and then I will be-
> come indeed the poet of my race. I feel this, Nora, as I
> write it. My body soon will penetrate yours, O that
> my soul could too! O that I could nestle in your
> womb like a child born of your flesh and blood ...

Elsewhere in his letters he called her 'my love, my star, my little strange-eyed Ireland', and finds in her image 'the beauty and doom of the race of whom I am a child'. For the most part, however, the masculine aspects of Ireland meant far more to him. His feelings about the country were conditioned first and foremost by his attachment to his father; in *Finnegans Wake* it is 'Sire-land' that the exile revisits in his dreams.

John Joyce was a staunch Parnellite, and no contemporary political event was ever again to impress his son anywhere near as forcibly as Parnell's fall, which took place when he was eight. The years which followed were frustrating ones for the nationalist movement; most Irishmen, according to Conor Cruise O'Brien, are still inclined to think of the interregnum between Parnell and the Easter Rising as a sort of 'featureless valley', and it was easy enough to feel at the time, as Joyce did, that Irish affairs were at a permanent tragicomic standstill. Nor would he have any truck with the cultural nationalism of the Gaelic League and the Irish literary revival: he first achieved notoriety in Dublin at the age of nineteen with 'The Day of the Rabblement', an article published at his own expense attacking the Irish Literary Theatre for surrendering to parochial pressures and staging plays based on Irish legend rather than the work of Continental masters like Ibsen and Hauptmann. And in his fiction, the two most memorable episodes dealing with Irish politics are a bitter epitaph on the old nationalism, and a derisive caricature of the new. 'Ivy Day in the Committee Room' shows a group of small-time politicians shuffling through their usual meaningless intrigues in the vacuum left by Parnell; the 'Cyclops' section of *Ulysses* lampoons the grotesque, bully-boy chauvinism of the fearsome Citizen. This is not quite the whole story; like Bloom, Joyce sympathised with Sinn Fein, and in Trieste, at a safe distance from Dublin, he wrote some forthright articles for the local press expounding the Irish case against England. (Given the significance which he generally attached to the question of names and namesakes, it argues a strong degree of personal involvement that with hundreds of years of history to choose from he should have selected as a symbol of Ireland's sufferings Myles Joyce, a Galway peasant who was wrongfully executed under particularly barbarous circumstances in 1882, the year he himself was born.) But eloquent though he could be on such topics as 'Il Fenianismo' and Home Rule, his decision to remain in exile speaks more eloquently still. Rightly or wrongly he continued to see in Irish life things to which he could never reconcile himself: back-stabbing, provincialism.

narrow-mindedness (and the fact that he wasn't actually married to Nora made matters worse). He had had to leave Ireland in order to be able to write about it, and he still had to elude the claims of nationalism if he was to celebrate the country on his own terms—with a passion which, to quote Stanislaus, was not 'the love of a patriot, which is an emotion for the market-place', but 'the comprehending love of an artist for his subject'.

At the start of his career, with the example of what Ibsen had accomplished for Norway in mind, Joyce saw his mission as being to Europeanise Irish literature, to make Ireland more aware of the great outside world. In the event, he was to make the great outside world aware of Ireland, as no previous Irish writer had done, or rather, aware of Dublin—its streets and quays, its lore and gossip, its history and landmarks. Joyce's Dublin (in *Ulysses*, at least) is as solid and full-flavoured as Dickens' London or Dostoievsky's St Petersburg. As with Dickens, it has produced its own brand of antiquarianism: the devotees who go on pilgrimages to the martello tower and the scholars who pore over *Thom's Directory of Dublin* for 1904 are the nearest modern equivalents to those old-fashioned Dickensians who used to busy themselves tracking down the coaching-inns of *Pickwick* or delving into the legal background of *Bleak House*. And their response is natural enough in its way: one obsession breeds another, and they have caught something of the intensity which Joyce himself brings to his most banal material, the intensity in his case of a man treasuring up the flotsam of his own past. For in reconstructing the Dublin scene he recalls not so much the urban sociologist or the photographic realist as the adolescent boy in Auden's poem:

> With the finest of mapping pens he fondly traces
> All the family names on the familiar places.

25

The inevitable corollary of this is that his picture of Irish life is often a very partial one. Whole aspects of his native city—social, economic, cultural, architectural— are either ignored or played down; and in any case, Dublin isn't Ireland. But although it is perhaps only for another Irishman to judge, in the end the world of his books certainly doesn't seem less representatively Irish than, say, Yeats's, or Synge's, or George Moore's. Even his role of exile has its representative value, reflecting as it does, however idiosyncratically, the situation of millions of Irishmen who had been forced to emigrate before him.

As his work grew more universal in scope, it also tended to grow if anything even more Irish in spirit, and in substance, too. He is reported to have told a friend that *Finnegans Wake* was about 'Finn lying dying by the river Liffey with the history of Ireland and the world cycling through his mind'. Although a lot of other descriptions would actually fit the book just as well, there can be no doubt that the *Wake* is saturated with a curious mixture of Irish history and mythology, with what a medieval romance writer might have called 'the matter of Ireland'. Finn—Finn MacCool, the principal hero of the southern cycle of ancient Irish legend, the slumbering giant on whose body Dublin rests—is H. C. Earwicker in his epic aspect. Earwicker also assumes in the course of the night the roles of Brian Boru, King Roderick O'Connor, St Lawrence O'Toole; and so many other references to the fabulous or semi-fabulous early periods of Irish history are woven into the *Wake* that Professor Vivian Mercier has been led to talk (in his excellent book *The Irish Comic Tradition*) of Joyce's 'new, almost Yeatsian attitude to Irish folklore', a far cry from 'The Day of the Rabblement' and his former hostility. This seems to me somewhat exaggerated : after all, *Finnegans Wake* takes its title from a raucous music-hall ballad of a kind which would surely have earned Yeats's iciest contempt, and Joyce valued the Tim Finnegan in his hero as much as the Finn. On Professor Mercier's own showing, his smattering of Gaelic meant less to him than a song like 'Phil the Fluter's Ball'. On the other hand Earwicker-as-Finn is no mere figment of the Celtic Twilight; he bulks in the imagination like a true pagan demigod. Joyce also makes extensive use of the Christian aspects of Irish antiquity, which find little or no place in the poetry of the Protestant-born Yeats. St Patrick is one of the most notable avatars of Shem, while cold-blooded Shaun is brilliantly pilloried in the legend of the ascetic St Kevin. Many other Irish themes and personalities are taken up seriously by Joyce for the first time : as Herbert Howarth has pointed out, for instance, the haughty Anglo-Irish Parnell—more Anglo than Irish in manner—is now joined in the pantheon by the far more robustly Irish figure of Daniel O'Connell (supposedly a distant connection of Joyce's paternal forebears). And even the Citizen could hardly complain of the lack of native content in a book which contains, among other things, the titles of almost all Tom Moore's 120-odd *Irish Melodies*, the names of some two hundred former Lord Mayors of Dublin, and innumerable references to every conceivable branch and twig of Irish literature from Bishop Berkeley to *The Colleen Bawn*.

It will be seen from all that has been said so far that when Stephen Dedalus, near the end of the *Portrait*, defiantly rejects the claims of family, fatherland, and Church, he is in fact naming at least two of what were to be Joyce's constant major themes. The question of religion is a more complicated one. Between them, Joyce's mother and his Jesuit schoolmasters ensured that he was given an intensely Catholic upbringing; as Prefect of the Sodality he was being groomed for a priestly vocation during adolescence, and the lasting intellectual influence of the Jesuits is apparent in his whole cast of mind. By the time he left school, however, he had lost his faith for good, and come to regard the grip exercised by the Church as one of the prime causes of Ireland's 'paralysis'. The strategically-placed opening story of *Dubliners*, 'The Sisters', described the death of an old, paralysed, spiritually bankrupt priest, a broken man, as seen through the eyes of a young boy who might once have been destined for the priesthood himself, but who still has a chance to escape. A later story, 'Grace', satirises the worldliness and complacency of smooth-spoken Father Purdon and his congregation of mildly penitent businessmen. In the *Portrait* Joyce's personal involvement naturally goes very much deeper. The main action of the book turns on Stephen's adolescent crisis of faith, and his sense of guilt, his longing for absolution, the impact of Father Arnall's hellfire sermon are all rendered with a power which suggests how much hold Catholicism still had over Joyce's imagination. At least one Catholic convert, Thomas Merton, has testified that it was a reading of the *Portrait* which first drew him towards the Church. But for Joyce himself there could be no going back. In Trieste, asked to fill in his religion on an application form for a job, he wrote 'Senza'—'without'; and there is nothing in either *Ulysses* or *Finnegans Wake* to indicate that he would subsequently ever have come up with a different answer. Given how many Dubliners swarm through *Ulysses*, the clergy are conspicuous by their relative absence, and of those priests who do appear, the most memorable, Father Conmee—in the early pages of the *Portrait*, the all-powerful, all-wise rector of Clongowes, Stephen's school—is shown as being as marginal to the real life of the book as the Viceroy, whose bland official progress through the city parallels his own. Nor are the saints' legends and ecclesiastical furnishings of the *Wake* matched by any comparable interest in the Church as a living, on-going institution. As a final gesture of disaffection from Rome on Joyce's part, the Earwickers in fact turn out to be Protestants.

Abandoning Catholicism, Joyce clung to a sacramental view of the world, with art taking the place of religion. This is more than a metaphor : Stephen's aesthetic theories in the *Portrait* are pieced together out of fragments of theology, while in his moods of self-exaltation towards the end of the book he comes dangerously close to suffering from messianic delusions. The Artist is also the Redeemer. The situation in *Ulysses* is more paradoxical : now it is Stephen himself, sterile and frustrated, who stands in need of redemption, and down-to-earth Bloom who has it in his power to redeem him. But Bloom in his turn needs to be redeemed, and it is only the artist who can save him by conferring immortality and transforming (or transubstantiating) his profane everyday world into a resplendent myth. *Ulysses* is crammed with messianic and biblical allusions—to Moses, to Elijah, above all to Christ; it is often hard while reading it to bear in mind that it doesn't represent the summit of Joyce's ambitions, that it didn't exhaust once and for all his urge to rival Holy Writ. But in retrospect the story of Bloomsday, the 'usylessly unreadable Blue Book of Eccles', merely hints at the vast allegorical designs and scriptural pretensions of *Finnegans Wake*. In the *Wake* Joyce aspires to the role of Blake's Bard, who 'Present, Past, and Future sees', and it seems tolerably clear that in some sense he believed he was engaged in creating a sacred text, an ultimate Book of Books.

How seriously are we to take all this? Discussing the Viconian structure of the *Wake* with Padraic Colum, Joyce told him : 'I don't take Vico's speculations literally, of course; I use his cycles as a trellis', and it would be pleasant to think that if pressed he would have given a similar account of the borrowings from Theosophy and the various other bits of esoteric mumbo-jumbo embedded in the book (and to a lesser extent in *Ulysses*, too). But one can't be sure. He was a superstitious man, notoriously impressed by portents and coincidences, ready to entertain the most bizarre occult fantasies; even his paternalistic mock-theology has a taint of superstition about it (and in any case, one can sense behind it a deeper, more truly religious impulse, a longing to be reunited with the natural order which transcends man-made systems, the elemental Nature which he tried to express through Molly and Anna Livia). On the whole, as with Yeats, it seems best to play down the occult aspects of his work wherever possible, while accepting that this must necessarily involve a certain amount of missing or misinterpreting the point. But one characteristic which can't be disregarded, since it is built into the very essence of the *Wake*, is his ability to equate his own experience with that of humanity at large, to treat it as though it were at once both unique and universal. Unlike a traditional mystic, he tries to attain the Absolute not by extinguishing his personality, but on the contrary by proclaiming it in every line he writes. As a small boy, puzzling over his place in the universe, Stephen Dedalus had reflected that 'it was very big to think about everything and everywhere. Only God could do that. He tried to think what a big thought that must be; but he could only think of God. God was God's name just as his name was Stephen.' In *Finnegans Wake* Joyce set out to play at being God without giving up the part of Stephen, without relinquishing his own identity. It was an impossible ambition, and to my mind it was more than anything else what made the *Wake* a doomed enterprise.

One last word of caution. In trying to penetrate beyond the myth of Joycean impersonality, or in trying to account for his literary aberrations, one is liable to uncover so much evidence of neurotic disturbance that it is important to remember that in the most basic terms his life was a success. He founded a family, and he wrote his books (setting equal store by both achievements). In the *Wake* Shem's house is mockingly referred to as 'the Haunted Inkbottle', a phrase which strikingly conjures up the murky obsessions which continued to plague Joyce until the end. But it also suggests, I think, the genie in the bottle, the creative power which he had at his command. For his readers what finally count are not the ghosts which haunted him, but the books in which he tried to exorcise them.

3 The Voyage Out

Like Stephen Dedalus, or like any adolescent growing up in the nineties with vague hankerings after literature, Joyce originally thought of himself as a poet. While he was still a schoolboy he wrote a collection of verses with the impeccably *fin de siècle* title of *Moods*, and during his university days he put together a second collection, *Shine and Dark*. Most of these early pieces have disappeared, but the handful which survive suggest that this is no very great loss: they are mawkish, derivative, absurdly high-flown. *Chamber Music* (written 1902–4, published 1907) represents a striking advance in technical sophistication; by the time he was twenty Joyce had studied the craftsmanship of Yeats, Verlaine and the Elizabethans to good effect. But his chosen literary persona was still remorselessly poetic, rather after the manner of Marchbanks in *Candida*, and the language of *Chamber Music* tends to be correspondingly archaic and fey. At best, the poems in the collection have a certain tremulous charm, or dimly foreshadow subsequent Joycean themes; at worst, they are pallid and sickly; for the most part they are conventional well-tailored lyrics, calculated to appeal to an Edwardian composer of 'art-songs' rather than a modern reader. There is far more feeling, and more true poetry, in the Swiftian octosyllabics of Joyce's outburst against his fellow Irish writers, 'The Holy Office' (1904), or in his later satirical broadside, 'Gas from a Burner' (1912).

In 'The Holy Office', written shortly after the first of the stories which were eventually to make up *Dubliners*,

Joyce let fly at the ethereal poets of the Celtic Twilight
in the name of an unflinching cathartic realism :

> *That they may dream their dreamy dreams*
> *I carry off their filthy streams ...*

He was also repudiating, by implication, the courtly
manner and the rarefied sentiments of *Chamber Music*
(much as he was to do in the passage in *Ulysses* where
Bloom's reflections on the acoustics of chamber-pots deliberately bring out the latent *double-entendre* in his earlier choice of title). After 1904, indeed, he was never
again to picture himself primarily as a poet, except in
sentimental moments. His lyric impulse lived on, to re-
assert itself in strange new contexts; no other twentieth-
century English writer was to do more to enlarge the
poetic possibilities of prose. But the fact remains that by
the time he left Ireland he had instinctively come to recognise that his true medium was fiction, not poetry. By
comparison with his major works, the autobiographical
poems in *Pomes Penyeach* (1927), his only collection of
verse after *Chamber Music*, are jottings in the margin,
semi-private souvenirs; although one might make an exception for 'Tilly', the reworked version of a poem originally prompted by the death of his mother, and also for
the equally haunting late lyric 'Ecce Puer' (1932), which
commemorates the birth of his grandson and the death
of his father a few weeks earlier. Joyce himself was the
first to acknowledge, rather wistfully, that 'Ecce Puer'
was an exception. Sending a copy to his friend Louis
Gillet, he added : 'You will tell me if you like it a little. I
am *papa mais pas poète.*'

In abandoning verse for prose, the young Joyce was
committing himself, in the first instance, to the for-
tuitous world of appearances, to the concrete, contin-
gent, imperfect here-and-now. Poetry, for the author of

Chamber Music, was an art of universals, evoking a timeless realm of archetypes and abstractions; fiction, for the author of *Dubliners*, was pre-eminently the art of particulars, of

> *Sydney Parade and Sandymount tram,*
> *Downes's cakeshop and Williams's jam.*

It was the novelist's task, and his privilege, to bow to circumstance, to insist on the validity of the passing moment, the mundane detail, the precise gesture or setting or intonation. But how were such moments to be redeemed from triviality, invested with a more-than-passing significance? Joyce began by trying to solve the problem head-on, in the 'Epiphanies' which he set down in his notebooks between 1900 and 1903: brief prose sketches, some of them lyrical and dreamlike, the majority recording without comment drab domestic scenes and banal everyday occurrences. An epiphany means 'a showing-forth', and Joyce believed that if he transcribed a moment of revelation, however outwardly commonplace, with sufficient care, he could make it yield up its full spiritual value. Such, at least, was the theory; but in practice those 'objective' epiphanies which survive are obstinately lifeless and undramatic (and, conversely, most of the subjective lyrical epiphanies lack shape and substance). A typical specimen, preserved in *Stephen Hero*, is the snatch of mumbled dialogue which Stephen overhears one evening as he passes a couple on the steps of a house in Eccles Street, 'one of those brown brick houses which seem the very incarnation of Irish paralysis'. Whatever private resonance their exchange may have had for Stephen at the time, for Joyce's readers, denied any further explanation, the incident is meaningless. It was to take more than an epiphany to penetrate the mysteries of Eccles Street. Ten years later Joyce was at last ready to do just that—the Blooms live in one of those brown brick houses, number seven; but first he had to undergo a long and tortuous voyage of self-discovery.

Stephen Hero itself marks a fresh beginning, a premature attempt to take stock of his early experience. It is very much a first novel, not least in its unselective sprawl: the section which survives, covering the hero's student years, is nearly five times as long as the corresponding section of the *Portrait of the Artist*. For anyone interested in Joyce's life, this is a self-evident gain. Episodes merely hinted at in the *Portrait* are described at length; instead of being relegated to an increasingly hazy background, Stephen's family and friends are allowed to exist in their own right. By comparison with the later book, too, there is something touching about the unguarded over-explicitness, the lack of Dedalean cunning. But none of this can make *Stephen Hero* a successful novel, or Stephen himself much more than a dummy on which Joyce has draped his own attitudes and opinions. The only immediate remedy, as fortunately Joyce saw, was to eliminate Stephen altogether and to concentrate on showing up the environment against which he had rebelled. Hence *Dubliners*.

With these tales of mean streets, the originality of Joyce's artistic vision declared itself unmistakably for the first time. Even today, after Hemingway, after the *New Yorker*, after innumerable practitioners of the oblique or laconic modern short story, it does not require any great effort of historical imagination to appreciate how clean a break with the whole clogged-up tradition of nineteenth-century English story-telling they represent. Nothing is redundant, and nothing is spelled out; we are expected to supply the missing pieces ourselves, to deduce the pattern of a career or the ramifications of a society from a few sparse narrative strokes. Similarly the language, ostensibly flat and neutral, in fact subtly mimics the moral conditions which it describes, by means of strategically-placed clichés, shabby-genteel euphemisms, jog-trot repetitions. Nor is there any sharp dividing-line between the stretches of deliberately trite dialogue and the ironically-inflected passages of reported speech, or for that matter between reported speech and descriptive comment. The narrator constantly slips into impersonating, not so much this or that character, as the collective voice of this or that social milieu—wheedling, boastful, hail-fellow, prim, sentimental, as the case may be. At times we even edge towards the burlesque narrative techniques of *Ulysses*, towards the anonymous blague of 'The Cyclops' and the tired cliché-mongering of 'Eumaeus'.

Some commentators have been tempted to read far more of Joyce's later manner than this back into *Dubliners*, combing the stories for hidden allegorical designs and recondite allusions. My own view is that the potential undercurrents of symbolism, whether Joyce intended them or not, are best disregarded, except where they impress themselves directly on the reader, without benefit of critical intervention. Thus, the broken chalice in 'The Sisters' emerges naturally from its immediate dramatic context as a symbol of violated integrity, while Joyce's writing is certainly taut enough for vibrations from the original use of the image to be still in the air when the young boy in 'Araby' talks metaphorically of the chalice which he bears through a hostile world. Symbolism of this order is both apt and unstrained. On the other hand it seems to me that nothing whatever is gained by being told, for instance, that the dour bank-official in 'A Painful Case' has no stomach for his corned beef and cabbage because his humour (in the medieval sense) is melancholic, and because Galen—according to the *Anatomy of Melancholy*—explicitly condemns corned beef as the worst possible food for a patient suffering from an ex-

cess of black bile. In the myth-laden
Ulysses this kind of esoteric flourish is
out of account, much as one would often
Dubliners it constitutes a mere incongruou
on the naturalistic surface.

Naturalism is a term of which critics hav   to
fight shy, at any rate when discussing authors whom
they admire. It has come to suggest the lumpish social
tract, the indiscriminate—and indigestible—slice of life,
the brooding asphalt-jungle melodrama with its framework of coarse pseudo-Darwinian determinism. *Dubliners* is none of these things, but it is an essentially
naturalistic work nevertheless—or rather, it is the product of an 'aesthetic' temperament applying itself to
naturalistic ends. And Joyce never swerves in his fidelity
to the disagreeable facts. However fastidiously he may
arrange or display his material, he keeps his eye steadily
trained on the world as he finds it: the waste lots, the
pub-crawls, the fusty interiors and the constricted lives
which they enclose.

The first three stories in the book, as he explained in
a latter to Stanislaus, were taken from his own childhood. Recounted in the first person, they share the common theme of disenchantment. A vocation for the
priesthood turns sour; a harum-scarum adventure is cut
short by the attentions of a seedy pervert; by the time the
boy manages to get to the Araby bazaar, with all its
promise of high romance, the show is over, and he is left
to wander disconsolately through the dark and glamour-
less hall. In the remaining stories, which (as he again explained to Stanislaus) are meant to deal successively with
the worlds of 'adolescence, maturity, and public life',
Joyce switches to the third-person, but continues to con-
fine himself almost exclusively to areas of which he has
intimate first-hand experience. Many of his characters
are based on relatives and acquaintances; others, as has

often been pointed out, represent partial projections of what he himself might have become if he had stayed in Dublin. Neurotic Duffy with his Nietzschean delusions, Little Chandler the frustrated poet, parasitic Lenehan, solid Martin Cunningham, Doran the clerk trapped into marriage—all of them in their different ways conjure up a James Joyce gone wrong. Not that this makes him extend any exceptional charity towards them, however. They are selves he is glad to discard, and they merge into the general morass of the life around them. For *Dubliners* is above all a work of rejection. Sullen or sluggish, ignoble or despondent, the citizens circulate to no purpose; the very rounds which they stand one another in the pubs come to sound like so many turns of the treadmill. If nothing which exactly deserves to be called tragic happens, neither does anything hopeful or exhilarating —and on every side there is evidence of petty degradation. As the indictment of an entire city, it ranks with Stendhal's unyielding verdict on Grenoble in *La Vie de Henri Brulard* : 'that town which I still hate, for it is there that I learned to know men'.

Given the single-mindedness of his revulsion, it is remarkable how adroitly Joyce managed to vary his artistic approach. Yet in the end he cannot altogether avoid monotony or succeed in disguising a certain cut-and-dried quality. The prose, for all its artfulness, tends to level off into an even drone; the characters, when we look back at them, have the flatness as well as the clarity of magiclantern silhouettes. In trying to maintain a stance of bleak detachment he was forced to suppress a great deal of his creative energy, as his subsequent development makes clear, and it is illuminating to recall in this connection that the idea of *Ulysses* first took shape in his mind as a short story, a possible addition to *Dubliners*. One need only think of how dim and unprepossessing a creature Bloom would look reduced to the proportions of an ironical ten-page sketch. And in retrospect, the presence in *Dubliners* of a number of characters who reappear in *Ulysses* serves as much as anything else to bring out how much richer and more flexible the treatment would be if the incidents which take place in the stories were transposed to the novel. True, once every so often there is a hint of ambivalent emotions, as in the sad little episode where the elderly, ugly kitchen-maid sings 'I dreamt that I dwelt in marble halls', or a scene which mildly anticipates Joyce's later blend of absurdity and pathos : the rambling sickroom conversation about religion in 'Grace', for instance. But such momentary flickers of warmth do not go very far towards dispelling the prevailing chill.

The one story which by common consent transcends these limitations is 'The Dead'. Coming as it does at the end of the book, it gathers up the themes of the preceding stories into a resonant grand finale; it also introduces for the first time a protagonist of something approaching Joyce's own intellectual calibre. All said and done, we are never in any danger of confusing Lenehan, Duffy, and the rest with their creator. At most, they are minikin reflections of certain isolated aspects of his personality. But Gabriel Conroy, the discontented university lecturer and literary journalist, is a far more considerable figure, and the gradual erosion of his egotistical defences is too complex and painful a process to be accomplished with a few deft ironies : it calls for elaborate dramatic counterpointing and delicate psychological insight. The felicities of the story have frequently been analysed, and it seems unlikely that future critics are going to find anything very new to say about the moral impact on Gabriel of the revelation that his wife's tears are being shed for a long-dead lover, or about such major architechtonic devices as the use of the snow to suggest, in the first instance, estrangement and isolation, then the lure of

heroic solitude, and finally, in the words of Richard Ellmann, 'the mutual dependency of living and dead'. But
since most critical comment has understandably been
devoted to the magnificent crescendo of the last few
pages, it is perhaps still worth emphasising how far
Joyce's ultimate success depends on the firm authority
with which he establishes the initial setting and the un-
sentimental tolerance which he accords his commonplace minor characters. Here, as nowhere else in *Dubliners*, the analogy sometimes made with Chekhov is
justified; here, too, for the first time in the book, Joyce
allows himself to be lavish—in his account of the conversation about opera-singers, for instance, or in his lov-
ing inventory of the food heaped up on the dinner-table,
or in the thick tangle of family history which he implies.
If the Morkan sisters' annual Christmas party is no
Dingley Dell idyll, neither is it an eerie *Totentanz*; and to
say flatly with Hugh Kenner that everyone in the story is
dead is to betray the fine balance which Joyce has
achieved, and the spirit in which he discriminates between mechanical gestures or moribund traditions and
the living impulses to which in spite of everything they
still bear witness.

In a sense, Joyce was running ahead of himself when
he wrote 'The Dead'. Younger and fiercer than Gabriel
Conroy, he was not yet ready to renounce the proud
intransigence which had inspired the other stories in
Dubliners—not, at least, until he had created as definitive a version of the romantic rebel as he had of the
society against which he was in revolt. The problem as it
now presented itself was how best to extract a valid
work of art from the crude ore of *Stephen Hero*, and the
apparently paradoxical solution which Joyce hit on was
to intensify rather than tone down the egoism of the
earlier work. In the *Portrait of the Artist*, hero and novel

are coextensive. Everything which happens to Stephen is registered in terms of his sensibility at that particular stage, while events are important purely in so far as they help to shape his inner development; the other characters only exist, as it were, when Stephen's around in the quad. Moreover, his superiority is now assumed rather than argued as it was in *Stephen Hero*. He is quite simply made of finer clay than his fellows, and the implications of his being called Dedalus in a world of Dolans and Lynches are reinforced by an elaborate system of imagery involving birds, water, and the Icarus legend generally. Yet the more arrogant of the two books is also artistically the more detached. In the pseudo-objective *Stephen Hero* Joyce is constantly pleading Stephen's case or nudging us into applauding his virtues; in the *Portrait*, on the other hand, he confines himself to hammering out an image and offering it for our inspection. We may approve or disapprove, but there at any rate it stands, plain for all to see.

To describe the book in these terms is not necessarily to endorse the famous distinction which Stephen draws in the last chapter between 'static' and 'kinetic' art, between art which 'arrests the mind' (as he thinks it should) and the inferior variety which plays directly on our emotions and moves us to 'desire or loathing'. If stasis simply means that the artist has remained in control of his materials, and avoided inflicting his designs upon us too palpably, well and good. But if the assumption is that ideally a work of literature ought to elicit as purely aesthetic a response as, say, a still life or a Persian carpet, then Stephen is involved in a major contradiction, since the whole tenor of the *Portrait* itself runs counter to any such theory. In the finest scenes of the novel—the Christmas dinner with its bitter quarrel over Parnell, the unjust pandybatting, the visit to Cork, Father Arnall's fearful sermons—we tremble with

Stephen as we might with a child in Dickens, and enter his feelings as deeply (or as kinetically) as those of a Dostoievskian raw youth. The intricacies of the symbolism and the closely calculated narrative shifts do nothing to diminish the emotional impact, any more than, say, the Arnall sermons are a mere clever pastiche because it turns out that, far from being written at white heat, they were to a considerable extent carefully adapted from a tract by a little-known seventeenth-century Italian Jesuit, Pinamonti's *Hell Opened to Christians*. We react to the preacher wholly in the context of Stephen's adolescent sexual guilt, and our reaction in turn helps to bring home the nature of Stephen's anguish—including its melodramatic aspects—as no amount of direct description could.

Few readers of the *Portrait*, once they have got the hang of Joyce's stylistic innovations, can have found much to quarrel with in the first two-thirds or so of the book. As a bewildered child, or as a schoolboy buffeted by the storms of puberty, Stephen is a victim who automatically enlists our support; it is only when he begins to assert himself and to proclaim his artistic creed that we start having doubts. If we are adolescents ourselves when we first come across the *Portrait*, we may possibly take him at his own valuation, but after that it is hard not to be repelled, or on occasion amused, by his posturing and his moist romanticism. He is utterly self-absorbed; his reveries are rendered in the over-exquisite accents of the House Beautiful; the one specimen of his poetry we are shown might almost have been written by Enoch Soames. And yet at the same time he is the undisputed hero of the piece, striding radiantly forward to embrace his destiny as the curtain falls.

How exactly are we to take all this? If we assume that Joyce completely identifies himself with Stephen, the final section of the book becomes an exercise in naive self-glorification, chiefly interesting for what it unconsciously reveals about the author's blind spots and immature yearnings. Anxious to acquit him of having perpetrated anything so disagreeable, a number of critics have gone to the opposite extreme in their interpretation, treating the *Portrait* as the deliberate and systematic exposé of a radically false attitude to life. Stephen's style betrays him because it is meant to; his absurdities and inadequacies supply the dry light of irony by which his grandiose gestures are to be judged. Depending on whether we prefer the satirical or the naturalistic variant of this approach, he is either a monster of conceit or the hapless product of a blighting environment, but in either case he is essentially sterile, and the principal characteristic which he shares with his exemplar Icarus is that he is heading for a fall. The portrait of the artist turns out to be the dissection of a second-rate aesthete.

A plausible case has more than once been constructed along these lines, and undoubtedly the idea of everything that Stephen says or does being held up for our unqualified approval is not one which will bear much inspection. There can be no mistaking the calculated manner in which his rhapsodisings are periodically set off against his unheroic behaviour or punctured by the irruption of crude Dublin reality. Yet despite this, the tone and over-all momentum of the book, in my experience at least, are not primarily those of a cautionary tale. If they were, and if Stephen's condition was really hopeless, Joyce could legitimately be taxed with a certain gratuitous cruelty : why dispatch so small a victim at such length, in such intimate detail, when he might have been decently disposed of in a short story? As it is, however, the *Portrait* is surely meant to leave us with equivocal feelings about its hero's potentialities. For much of the time Stephen embodies an aspect of Joyce's nature which he repeatedly punished in his books but which he could never finally quell: the egoarch, the poseur with a smack of Hamlet, the Narcissist who dedicated his first extended work (a play written at the age of eighteen and subsequently lost) 'to My own Soul'. But he also represents Joyce by virtue of his unaccommodating ideals and his restless imagination: even the purple patches hold out the promise of a more authentic, more distinctive lyricism. And he has the courage of his immaturity, which means having the capacity to grow and change, not being afraid of a plunge into the unknown. Whether he will ultimately justify his presumptuousness and succeed in writing his masterpiece is an open question as the book ends, but given his youth and his vulnerability it is a question which would scarcely arise at all if he had not armoured himself against the claims of conventional society with a defiantly romantic and Promethean conception of the artist's calling.

Richard Rowan, the artist-hero of *Exiles*, is a much less ambiguous figure. An Irish writer with a common-law wife called Bertha, paying a visit home to Dublin after nine years of self-imposed exile in Italy, he stands very close to Joyce as he was at the time the play was written—so close, indeed, that Joyce can never quite see him for the cold fish he is. Viewed through less partisan eyes, however, there is something peculiarly repellent about his morbid probing into other people's motives and his assumption that the world revolves around his own perverse needs. A joyless prima donna, he seems determined, while ostensibly acting in the name of freedom and enlightenment, to make everyone in his orbit as uneasy and frustrated as he is himself: never was there a less magnificent obsession than his craving for his wife to be unfaithful to him—half masochistically, half so that he can enjoy the moral advantage. We are a long way from Joyce's master, Ibsen, and not just in terms of theatricality: the stilted language and shadowy characterisation reflect a deeper failure than one of dramatic technique. Coming as it does immediately after the *Portrait*, the play is a sad anti-climax, and the best that can be said for it is that it is a retreat *pour mieux sauter*, a turning back to deal with unresolved personal problems. Joyce himself, in the face of a general lack of enthusiasm, continued to regard it as a major achievement: no doubt he had invested too many emotions in it to admit otherwise. But even while he was writing it a sounder instinct was enabling him to see the humour of his neurotic difficulties and prompting him to break out of the insulated, self-centred little world of Richard Rowan into the broad comic expanses of *Ulysses*.

4   In the Heart of the Hibernian Metropolis

I

Reduced to its simplest terms, *Ulysses* is the story of a chance encounter between two men who have been wandering around Dublin all day, and its possible life-enhancing repercussions. One of them is a none-too-successful advertising canvasser, the other an as-yet unproven artist—Stephen Dedalus, back home from his first flight abroad with his wings clipped and with a new sense of bitterness weighing him down. He is racked by guilt at the thought of his dead mother and estranged once and for all from his disreputable father; he feels intolerably hemmed in; the coarse, materialistic envious outside world, which he could afford to banter with in the days of Cranly and Lynch, now presents a far more formidable threat to his peace of mind in the person of plump Buck Mulligan. True, Joyce still takes care to let him outshine his acquaintances in literary debate, while his interior monologues reveal more than we could ever previously have guessed about the witty, volatile, audacious qualities of his intellect. He has also learned to ridicule the more flamboyant of his own pretensions. But his self-mockery has a hysterical edge to it, and he is plainly in the grip of a desperate personal crisis. Only a spiritual rebirth can save him—and it is in the maternity hospital, appropriately enough, that the chance of one is extended to him when he finally meets Leopold Bloom.

At first sight Bloom seems an improbable saviour. A man of no particular attainments, he is generally presented in a comic light and in unsparing physical close-up. He is also a veteran cuckold, an emasculated husband, a bungler, a slightly pathetic and slightly absurd social misfit. What, then, does he have to offer Stephen? Generous practical assistance, which makes him unusual, but hardly unique. Friendship, since he sees in Stephen the grown-up son he might one day have had if his own son hadn't died when he was a few days old—but the disparities between the two men are too great for this to be more than a wistful dream. Without his benevolent impulses, no doubt, contact would never have been established in the first place; but his real gift is the example of his personality and his power to endure. If Stephen can learn to appreciate him, to enter into his feelings, to see him for what he is, he will have gained access to his own pent-up humanity and found his true subject as a writer.

Whether he succeeds we are never in my view meant to know for sure. Many of Joyce's most illuminating critics from Edmund Wilson onwards have assumed that he does, that, in Mr Wilson's words, 'it is certain that Stephen, as a result of this meeting, will go away and write *Ulysses*', and that this act of self-begetting is the triumph towards which the design of the novel irresistibly tends. Attractive though such a reading is, however, it is useful to be reminded by a sceptical commentator like William Schutte (in *Joyce and Shakespeare*) that there is no direct evidence for it in the book itself, and that there are a good many incidents which seem to point the other way. Mr Schutte cites, for example, the moment when Stephen and Bloom gaze together into the mirror and see the features of Shakespeare reflected back—a Shakespeare 'rigid in facial paralysis'. If their qualities could really be fused, they would form a creative unity, but their limitations keep them impotently apart. Yet I think that Mr Schutte is further from the truth than the 'optimists' whom he sets out to refute when he goes on to conclude that Stephen's character has set like plaster, that it is too late for him to understand the Blooms of this world. On the contrary, the possibility of redemption has now been held out to him; it is what he will make of it that remains to be seen. And there is at least one good reason for Joyce not to be more explicit than this. Far from concealing himself behind the book, he makes his presence felt through innumerable technical interventions (the parodies, and so forth), in order to distance his characters and control the reader's response. If he were then to identify Stephen too positively with the Joyce of 1904, he would be in danger of appearing to boast openly about how far he had come, how decisively he had outgrown his youthful weaknesses. Instead, he discreetly leaves us to draw our own tentative conclusions.

So, too, with Bloom, although here the scope for change is much more limited. The meeting with Stephen may conceivably help to reinvigorate his marriage (his request for Molly to bring him breakfast the next day is a hopeful sign, her response somewhat less so), and it undoubtedly fortifies his morale to share confidences with the bearer of higher cultural values than those he has encountered most of the day in newspaper office, thoroughfare, pub, brothel. But the whole point about him is that he can't be fundamentally transformed, that he has learned to recognise the limits within which he is free to operate. As a sun-god he must keep wheeling through the same eternal round (Joyce's astronomy is pre-Copernican); as a man he must resign himself to a circumscribed quotidian existence. At the end of the *Portrait of the Artist* Stephen, spellbound by a vision of beckoning arms and voices, cries 'Welcome, O life!' Bloom is committed to the more difficult business of living from day to day, snatching small victories, practising unspectacular virtues, doing his best to alleviate habitual burdens.

It may be that we have been led astray by Joyce's irony if we view his hero as sympathetically as this. Early readers of *Ulysses*, still trying to digest its technical novelties and encouraged by the kind of praise it received from Eliot and Pound, were often inclined to see it as an extended tour of the Waste Land or a vast sottisier in the tradition of Flaubert; and although this interpretation has tended to fall out of favour in recent years, it still has some powerful and ingenious adherents. As in the case of critics who argue for a wholly ironical reading of the *Portrait*, in the end one can only argue back out of one's own experience of the book—with the added consideration that what has already been said about the elaborate heartlessness in which such an approach to the adolescent Stephen would implicate Joyce applies even more forcibly here. If Bloom were meant to be nothing more than a representative specimen, the walking embodiment of degraded modern mass-culture, then he should have been kept within the confines of *Dubliners*, as Joyce originally intended; to reveal the microscopic workings of his mind and to expose his every passing cliché or banality is to sentence him to death by a thousand cuts. In fact it is one of the great achievements of *Ulysses* to demonstrate as no previous novel had done the sheer density of the individual's mental life, the incredibly rapid succession and complexity of thoughts as they swarm past. And this plenitude gradually takes on a moral aspect; faced with such superabundance and so much inconsistency we surely ought to be a little more chary than we were before of passing simple definitive judgements on other people.

Moreover, Bloom and Stephen are not just isolated figures in a frozen tableau: they stand in as dynamic a relationship to each other as Don Quixote and Sancho Panza. They are spirit and flesh, if we like, or idealist and realist, or artist and bourgeois—but the pattern can't be reduced to a single motif. At one level the novel presents a comic version of the oedipal triangle, with Bloom as a dethroned, impotent, clownish father-figure, who virtually invites Stephen to supplant him in the marriage-bed. (It is worth noting in this connection, although Joyce himself doesn't dwell on it, that the roll-call of Molly's alleged former lovers in the 'Ithaca' questionnaire includes the name of Stephen's actual father, Simon Dedalus.) From another standpoint Bloom is the surrogate on whom Joyce had no qualms about heaping the psycho-sexual aberrations and indignities which he couldn't quite bring himself to attribute directly to Stephen; and he was able to do this, as Lionel Trilling has observed, because Bloom is in some ways felt to be a child, with a child's essential innocence. Yet he is also far more adult than Stephen—the novel is rich enough to sustain such paradoxes comfortably—and by virtue of his deeper immersion in life a model, however imperfect, of what Stephen can and should become. This in fact seems to me the most important link between the two characters. It is not quite the same as the father-and-son relationship, which can easily be made too much of, or at any rate taken too literally. For one thing, Bloom, a mere thirty-eight, is not really old enough to play the part of Stephen's father convincingly; for another, Stephen, though still obsessed by his parents, has reached the age when sons are normally starting to move forward towards fatherhood themselves. And Bloom's significance is that he can help him to release, not only the frustrated artist locked up inside him, but the potential husband and father too, the *papa* as well as the *poète*. It is this above all, I believe, which prompted Joyce to set the action of *Ulysses* on June 16th, 1904, the day on which

Nora Barnacle first went out with him and he took the path towards marriage.

That Bloom is neither a moral nor an intellectual paragon is a point which scarcely needs to be laboured : his backslidings and his disorganised notions are a major source of comedy in the book. 'Prove that he loved rectitude from his earliest youth,' demands the anonymous interrogator in 'Ithaca', and the response is a ludicrous jumble of his discarded religious beliefs and bygone political allegiances. As for his humanitarian ideals, they would be more immediately impressive if they were not so often couched in the language of tired newspaper-editorials. Yet the more we get to know about him, the more he justifies Joyce's description of him as quite simply 'a good man', in the sense of being basically a man of good will. When he yields to mean or servile impulses (as he sometimes does) we feel that he is falling below his own level; far more frequently, and more characteristically, he reveals himself as patient, considerate, dependable after a fashion, charitably inclined. And whatever label we use to sum up this unpretentious social morality, it is something which Stephen with all his imagination still has to learn. Contrasting Dedalus as poet with Bloom as moralist, I am reminded of a remark of Heine's about Hellenism and Hebraism, to the effect that 'being Greek is a young man's game; one ages into being a Jew'. Closer home, the difference between the two men's outlook also recalls Stephen's mother at the end of the *Portrait*, praying that one day her son will understand 'what the heart is and what it feels'. Not that there is any question of Bloom's goodness being purely instinctual, all heart and no head. It is, on the contrary, intimately bound up with his particular kind of intelligence—with his shrewdness, his sense of proportion, his lively curiosity about other people and his ability to put himself in their shoes. He is a thoughtful man, in both senses of the word; he also has a humorous awareness of the follies flourishing around him which makes him at least as much a critic of his society's values as their un-witting representative. And although *Ulysses*, like its author, has some highly irrational moments, it is not finally to be included among the modernist classics which declare war on reason in the name of Yeatsian passion or Lawrentian primitivism. The dark gods of 'Circe' are seen as demons to be cast out, and in so far as Bloom is meant to stand for mankind in general he is very much Homo sapiens, never more himself than when he is putting two and two together.

Any attempt to make a modern Everyman out of him, however, must be sharply qualified on at least two counts. In the first place, he is certainly not a little man in the tradition of Chaplin or Mr Polly or the Good Soldier Schweik. As *Ulysses* has ceased to be the preserve of the avant-garde, there has been an increasing tendency to present him as though he were—it can be seen at its most sugary in Joseph Strick's movie; but while such a reading may on balance be preferable to the older Flau-bertian or Waste Land interpretation, it completely leaves out of account the traces of scorn and even dis-taste which are mingled with Joyce's affection for Bloom, and the element of ice-cold detachment in the book as a whole. Bloom is usually amiable and some-times admirable, but at no point, I would say, could he be called lovable. Second, and more important, the very qualities which do enable him to retain our sympathy over such a distance, and which make his running com-mentary on the day's events so penetrating and amusing, also serve to set him apart from the miscellaneous com-mon crowd, from Everyman as personified by the hangers-on in Davy Byrne's bar or the carnivores in Burton's restaurant. It may be that if we were allowed to explore the minds of these lesser characters we would find that they react to life with an equally vivid internal poetry, but there is nothing within the terms of the novel itself to suggest that they do, and a great deal to confirm Bloom's status as a sensitive outsider. He has 'a touch of the artist', as Lenehan remarks, and his affinities with Stephen become steadily more apparent as the book proceeds. Both men are engaged in trying to make sense of their lives; each of them has to contend with a thrusting, coarse-fibred usurper in the shape of Blazes Boylan and Buck Mulligan respectively. Bloom speaking up for Love in Kiernan's saloon is as isolated as Stephen lecturing on Shakespeare in the National Library—and if he cuts a sorrier figure, it is partly because he provides a more appropriate vehicle for Joyce's masochism and self-pity. He is also alienated twice over on account of his race: cut off from his fellow-Jews, but never quite accepted by the Irish as one of themselves.

Yet however deeply such traits modify our picture of Bloom as a representative citizen and *père de famille*, they don't cancel it out. Joyce's triumph is to strike a balance—a more successful balance than one would have thought possible—between his persistent sense of himself as a lonely outcast and his growing readiness to acknowledge how much he had in common with ordinary inartistic humanity. And one consequence is a vague but unmistakable liberal slant to the book which is not at all characteristic of the high modernist tradition, while at the same time meaning far more than it would in a more conventional literary context: the platitudes of middlebrow fiction take on a new dramatic interest when they have to be fought for, put to the ingeniously-devised test, reaffirmed in the face of strong contrary pressures. In its undoctrinaire way, in fact, *Ulysses* is among the most democratic of modern novels, and not the less so because it travels the long way round in order to arrive at its democratic conclusions.

'One of the aspects of *Ulysses* that always pleases me,' wrote Joyce's friend Frank Budgen, 'is its popular character. It bears a resemblance to those old popular songs which tell of tragic happenings to a jolly tune and a ringing chorus of tooralooralay.' This is an aspect which must be quickly apparent to any reader of the book, but one which has seldom been done justice to by the commentators, intent as they are on more esoteric or problematic matters. (Mr Budgen himself is an honourable and eloquent exception.) Yet although demotic doesn't necessarily imply democratic, what I have loosely described as the book's implicit liberalism would add up to very little without Joyce's constant use of colloquial, mass-produced and plebeian materials. As much as anything it is popular culture which keeps Bloom in contact with his fellows, and which makes *Ulysses* the portrait of a city as well as of an individual.

The most pervasive popular element is provided by Joyce's close reliance on the informal spoken word : in almost every episode the language is heavily overlaid with slang, shop-talk, catchphrases, nicknames, shorthand expressions, all the idiomatic rags and tatters of everyday speech. Music-hall refrains and Palm Court lyrics contribute substantially to the general atmosphere; so do Bloom's professional preoccupations. Some of the novel's most striking motifs are taken straight from advertising —the Hely's sandwich-men, Alexander Keyes and his crossed keys, the jingle about Plumtree's Potted Meat— while one entire episode is set in a newspaper office and punctuated by phantom headlines designed to illustrate the shift in style from Late Victorian Orotund ('IN THE HEART OF THE HIBERNIAN METROPOLIS') to Early Twentieth-Century Aggressive ('ITHACANS VOW PEN IS CHAMP'). Other sources of mass culture or urban folklore on which Joyce draws include popular science, romantic novelettes, faded daguerreotypes, familiar quotations, pantomimes, riddles, topical jokes, sport ... But rather than go on, let me quote someone else's catalogue :

> I loved absurd pictures, inscriptions over doorways, stage scenery, fairground paintings, signboards, cheap coloured prints; out-of-date literature, church Latin, pornographic books full of spelling mistakes, the kind of novels our grandmothers used to enjoy, children's story-books, old operas, nonsensical refrains, simple rhythms.

This might almost be Joyce speaking; it is in fact a passage from Rimbaud's *Une Saison en enfer*, and a reminder that long before *Ulysses* avant-garde writers in France were exploiting the artistic possibilities—poetic and satirical alike—of popular entertainment and the kind of miscellaneous cultural bric-à-brac which clutters up the life of urban man. Among English novelists, however, there were no major precedents at the time Joyce was writing—unless one goes all the way back to Dickens, an even more original poet of the city, who in this respect as in many others anticipated his kaleidoscopic and impressionistic techniques. (Joyce himself seems to have remained unaware of the affinity; at any rate, according to Stanislaus he could never be induced to take an interest in Dickens's work.)

That *Ulysses* is shot through with borrowings from popular culture, everyone recognises; it is the use to which Joyce intended to put such material which is open to dispute. The most commonly expressed view, I suppose, is that he was trying to illustrate as concretely as possible the trivial and degraded fragmentation of modern existence. 'The metropolis is rank with forms of *negative vitality* ... James Joyce, in *Ulysses*, projected this phantasmal state: he showed the mind of Leopold Bloom regurgitating the contents of the newspapers and the advertisement, living in a hell of unfulfilled desires, vague wishes, enfeebling anxieties, morbid compulsions and dreary vacuities: a dissociated mind in a disintegrated city: perhaps the normal mind of the world metropolis.' This is a passing reference by Lewis Mumford in *The Culture of Cities*, and one which could be matched many times over from other sources—with good reason, since it reflects feelings which must regularly assail any reader of *Ulysses* as the unlovely details accumulate, even those readers who find Bloom basically sympathetic. Nor does Joyce simply dissect the subject-matter of mechanised culture; he also reproduces its characteristic tempo, its discontinuities and exclamation-marks, the ways in which it has invaded the modern psyche and disrupted long-established patterns of experience. Small wonder that Marshall McLuhan has claimed him as a major precursor, or that he sometimes achieves effects akin to Pop Art, transposing and enlarging journalistic motifs as a means of bringing out the bright harsh indifference of mass-publicity.

At the same time one can make him seem more prophetic than he really was by reading back into *Ulysses* the attitudes of a later period. Dublin in 1904 was only on the fringe of a 'world metropolis' which was itself far less tightly organised than it is today, and it seems a little hard to visit all the sins of Admass on poor Bloom, who had never heard of Hollywood or seen a supermarket and who was afraid of ending his days in a workhouse. Joyce himself was keenly aware of the rapid growth of mass-communications which took place within his own lifetime, and the Pop Art element is much stronger in *Finnegans Wake*, reflecting as it does the new media and the more powerful publicity-machines of the twenties and thirties. The *Wake* contains what must be among the earliest descriptions in any novel of television ('the bairdboard bombardment screen'), while at one point, juggling with the sacred initials HCE, Joyce even manages to anticipate the ubiquitous soup-tins of Andy Warhol, though he gets the wrong brand: 'Heinz Cans Everywhere'. In *Ulysses*, on the other hand, Madison Avenue is still undreamed-of, and we are firmly anchored in an early Edwardian, semi-provincial, lower-middle-class world which looks positively homely in the light of later developments.

Quite apart from the question of anachronistic distortions, however, there seem to me good grounds for dissenting from the idea that Joyce's attitude to Bloomsday culture was uniformly negative and sardonic. For one thing, he is at some pains to show good and bad, high and low mixed up together (admittedly a task made easier for him, in a novel in which music plays such a large part, by the unusually eclectic musical tastes of Dubliners of his father's generation). For another, his popular culture really *is* a culture, rather than a social critic's artificial construct: it is the element in which most of his characters live and the medium through which they express their feelings. This inevitably tempers the judgements which it might otherwise invite. The inferior artistic quality of a song like 'Those Lovely Seaside Girls', for instance, is not the only thing worth noting about it after it has woven itself into Bloom's thoughts about Molly and Boylan, about his daughter, about Gerty MacDowell, about death, until 'your head it simply swurls'.

One final consideration, equally important, is that Joyce himself took a good deal of pleasure in the kind of ephemera which float through Bloom's mind. The music-hall songs, scraps of doggerel and so forth are not mere research-material, specimens to be picked up with a pair of tweezers and held at arm's length; they represent one of his own spontaneous interests. A somewhat ambivalent interest, no doubt, often fenced around with irony, but an exhilarating one, too. The fact that Joyce felt compelled to play down this aspect of his character when he wrote *Dubliners* and the *Portrait* is one of the things which helps to account for the relatively close-cropped quality of those two books, although there are glimmerings in them of what is to come ; the glimpse of the servant-girl singing 'Rosie O'Grady' is arguably a more convincing epiphany than the famous vision of the girl wading on the beach, or would be if Stephen didn't turn away from it to lose himself in an incense-wreathed Pateresque trance. And much of the vitality of *Ulysses* is borrowed from popular material which it half-mocks. Whether it is judged to be 'negative vitality' depends on one's interpretation of the book as a whole, and of Bloom's significance in particular; but certainly there is very little biographical evidence to suggest that Joyce was either a purist or a puritan in such matters. What does emerge clearly, on the other hand, is the extent to which his enthusiasms remained those of his childhood and adolescence, or those associated with his father. As late as 1936, for instance, he was writing to his friend Constantine Curran, asking him to ransack the Dublin music shops for information about local music-hall stars of the nineties and the libretti of old Dublin panto-mimes : material which he partly wanted in connection with his work on the *Wake*, but which according to Curran he also cherished on its own account. There are many traces of this minor obsession in *Ulysses*, some of them so heavily concealed that they can hardly have gratified anyone except the author himself. Even a detail such as Bloom's drowsy rigmarole about Tinbad the Tailor and Whinbad the Whaler, which has exercised many commentators, turns out—thanks to the researches of Professor Robert Martin Adams—to contain direct echoes of a Christmas pantomime which Joyce was almost certainly taken to see when he was ten or eleven years old.

An attachment to childhood as powerful as this plainly runs the risk of turning sentimental, and sentimentality is one of Joyce's constant temptations. Here again one thinks of Dickens, although there is a more specifically Irish lilt to Joyce's nostalgia, the vibrant emotional note —touching and tender when it comes off, lush or histrionic when it doesn't—which so often steals into the art of oppressed peoples. (Yet another reason, incidentally, why Joyce must have found the idea of Bloom's Jewishness congenial.) All those references to Tom Moore in the *Wake*—and there are dozens of others in *Ulysses*—are a salute to a kindred spirit as well as an extended joke; and while Joyce's affinities with Swift are something which critic after critic has rightly stressed, I don't think he was being merely testy when he told Padraic Colum, who had been praising Swift's work for its intensity, that there was more true intensity in a single passage of Mangan's. Not his considered judgement, of course: Swift was one of his masters, and a major presence in the *Wake*. But it does seem to me fair to say that the author of 'Dark Rosaleen' touched a chord in his nature which Swift could never reach. And he was susceptible to weepier things still—rather endearingly, but at some cost to his prose style. There are damp patches in all his books, including *Ulysses* and the *Wake*, which call to mind Yeats's comment on *A Shropshire Lad*: 'a mile further and all had been marsh'.

No one was more aware of his maudlin or rhapsodical tendencies than Joyce himself; and much of his comic genius went into lampooning them. Bloom's sorrows become a theme for burlesque almost as soon as they are set down; the birdlike girl on the beach in the *Portrait*, with 'her skirts kilted boldly about her waist', is transformed into Gerty MacDowell; gushing sentiments are exaggerated and distorted until they start looking farcical or downright gruesome. But while self-parody was an essential safety-valve for Joyce, to some extent the warmth and colour of *Ulysses* are bound up with the impulses which he parodied. What ultimately saves the book from going soft at the centre is not so much the straight satire, in fact, as the firmness of the characterisation—above all Joyce's fully rounded and realistic conception of Bloom.

III

We began this chapter by considering *Ulysses* largely as though it were a conventional work of fiction, looking at it in terms of plot and character rather than in the light of its symbolism and its revolutionary techniques. This is, I believe, the most profitable point of departure, but pushed too far such an approach would create a hopelessly misleading impression. For the power of the book lies in its poetry, and in an exuberance which is inseparable from Joyce's daring complexities of presentation.

Of all his innovations, the most celebrated and the most immediately striking is his systematic use of a device for which there were only fitful or minor precedents, the interior monologue. Our first reaction is likely to be that this is less a technique than a deliberate rejection of technique, in the interests of verisimilitude : never before have the fluid and erratic processes of the mind been so faithfully rendered. As we grow acclimatised to *Ulysses*, however, it becomes clear that Joyce was far from attempting anything as inartistic—or, indeed, as impossible—as the direct transcription of thought. The soliloquies, although they have their rough

edges, are carefully structured and edited, as S. L. Goldberg demonstrates in his excellent discussion of the
whole question in *The Classical Temper*, pointing out,
for example, how skilfully Joyce uses the paragraph as a
dramatic unit. Mr Goldberg also clears up another common misconception about the stream of consciousness,
the idea that it is an essentially passive recording-process.
In fact both Bloom and Stephen bring an active intelligence and imagination to bear on the sense-data which
come flooding in on them : their thoughts, to quote
'Tintern Abbey', are a mixture of 'what they half create,
and what perceive'.

One further point about the interior monologue deserves to be stressed : in patenting the device, Joyce
didn't forget the switch which turned it off. The possibilities which it opened up for him were so exciting at
one level that he might easily have been trapped by
them at another, and lured into presenting the entire
action of the novel through the medium of Bloom's or
Stephen's individual sensibility. From the very beginning, however, he reserves the right to slip in and out of
either man's mind at will, interspersing soliloquy with
dialogue and stage-direction; and after he has established
their characteristic (and very different) rhythms of
thought in three episodes apiece, he begins to assert his
auctorial presence far more blatantly, with the un-
attached headlines in 'Aeolus'. After this the separate episodes, which have up till now been distinguished from
one another simply by mood, setting and a not very
obtrusive symbolism, turned into violently contrasting
exercices de style. We move from the maze of 'The
Wandering Rocks' to the Sirens' fugue, and then on to
the mock-epic of 'The Cyclops'; the element of parody
deepens, and we are offered (among other things) an
expressionist drama, a pseudo-scientific catechism, a
Peg's Paper novelette and a comic history of English

prose. Nor would a full list of the major shifts in narrative technique give one much idea of all the minor variations.

These might roughly be classified under five main heads:

thematic—patterns of imagery, internal allusions, external parallels, the reintroduction or fragmentation of previously-established motifs

mimetic—onomatopoeia, imitative rhythms, violations of normal word-order and other devices designed to make the language enact what it describes

cinematic—the literary equivalents of close-ups, flash-backs, slow motion sequences, tracking shots, jump cuts and so forth; not that the cinema was in any way a direct source of inspiration, but it does provide the neatest analogy for Joyce's dynamic handling of space and constantly shifting angle of vision

poetic—imaginative wordplay, condensed syntax, startling metaphors, abrupt juxtapositions: poetic effects, that is to say, in the spirit of symbolist or post-symbolist poetry

centrifugal—jokes, interruptions, false clues, marginal erudition, Rabelaisian catalogues, tricks after the fashion of *Tristram Shandy* intended to overflow the framework of the story and draw attention to the artificial nature of the fictional medium itself.

These categories often coincide, however, and they are certainly not meant to cover every aspect of the case: no brief schema could hope to do that.

What such a summary can make clear is the extent to which Joyce's experimental techniques pull in two directions at once. Many of them serve to heighten the surface realism of *Ulysses* and to reinforce the impression of accurate psychological notation. Many others do just the opposite : they are deliberately obtrusive, anti-illusionist, the calculated firework displays of a virtuoso. And no one is going to get the best out of the novel unless he is to some extent ready to accept such displays for their own sake, for their wit and inventiveness, without worrying unduly about how far they can be accommodated to traditional fictional procedures. They are in fact among Joyce's chief claims to the title of modern, or modernistic, master. For *Ulysses* came at an explosive moment in Western culture, at a time when artists were dismembering ideals which had prevailed since the Renaissance, importing and concocting exotic techniques, taking technique itself for their subject—and Joyce is as commanding a representative of this phase in literature as Picasso is in painting.

Analogies between literature and the other arts only hold good up to a certain point, however : words have meanings, and the idea of a novel as pure technique is a contradiction in terms. And while the novelistic aspects of *Ulysses* are not in doubt, many critics have complained that the technical innovations are often at odds with them. With this I would agree, except to add that far from being a weakness, the resulting tension is generally a fruitful one—that characters are deliberately played off against techniques, and not merely for comic effect, either. Bloom is exposed to surrealist ridicule in 'Circe', ruthlessly parodied in 'Eumaeus', put through the mangle in 'Ithaca', and in every case he survives the ordeal. Not that Joyce is uniformly successful in this respect : personally, for instance, I find the grotesquely namby-pamby vision of the dead Rudy at the end of 'Circe' unnecessarily demeaning, too inconsistent with what we already know and feel about Bloom. But in the end, despite such lapses, Bloom's humanity remains proof against lurid mutations, dismissive judgements,

even against the more desiccated sections of 'Ithaca'.
First and last he is the same man : an identity crisis is
not part of his 'modern' luggage. And in its own way the
language of the novel proves equally resistant to fundamental change. Take 'The Sirens', the episode where
literature aspires towards the condition of music as never
before, where the small talk of the Ormond bar and the
mid-afternoon activities of Blazes Boylan resound with
staccato and *glissando* and *appoggiatura* effects. If we
suppose that Joyce was solemnly trying to find the exact
verbal equivalents of musical forms, then he was engaged on as dubious and foredoomed an experiment as
hostile critics have claimed; but surely it fits the facts
better to assume that he was consciously exploiting the
impossible nature of such an ambition. Much of the
comedy (and the odd beauty) of the episode rises out of
the way in which language is *not* like music, especially
when it carries the humdrum connotations of workaday
narrative prose. In poetry, perhaps, *de la musique avant
toute chose*; but in a novel, or at any rate in a novel like
Ulysses, bald deaf Pat the waiter and bending, suspend-
ing Miss Douce the garter-twanging barmaid remain
obstinately and bizarrely untransformed as they are put
through their musical paces.

Technical versatility on the Joycean scale exacts its
price, and *Ulysses* cannot altogether be defended against
the charge that it lacks organic unity. For a writer whose
roots were largely in the romantic tradition, indeed,
Joyce often displayed a surprisingly mechanistic cast of
mind. But the fact that the events and personages of the
novel are not overwhelmed by the variations in technique means that the narrative is a good deal less dis-
jointed than at first appears, since it is above all the story
of Bloomsday which binds it together. And even the
technical twists and stratagems confer a certain paradoxical consistency : they reveal the guiding hand of an

author who bears far more resemblance to Homer's hero than Bloom does, in the sense of being a man of many devices. As Wyndham Lewis remarked long ago, the very title *Ulysses* suggests 'a romantic predilection for guile' on the part of Joyce himself.

Is there a deeper unity to the novel than this? If there is, we must plainly look for it at the level of myth, and no aspect of *Ulysses* has given rise to more discussion than its mythic or mythopoeic elements. It is a discussion, moreover, which has grown steadily more elaborate across the years. In the twenties, when Eliot singled out Joyce's resuscitation of myth as his most important contribution to contemporary literature, what he principally had in mind was simply the way in which *Ulysses* puts the *Odyssey* to ironical use. At the beginning of the thirties Stuart Gilbert, writing with the benefit of Joyce's co-operation, demonstrated just how extensive some of the Homeric parallels actually are; he also disclosed the novel's emblematic groundplan—with each episode allotted its particular colour, bodily organ, etc.—and hinted at the presence of rich layers of meaning which had gone largely undetected up till then, borrowings from theology, mysticism, folklore and much else besides. For Mr Gilbert, 'every detail in *Ulysses* is significant', and since his pioneering exegesis scores of other commentators have tackled the novel in the same thorough-going spirit. It has been combed for ingenious double meanings and ransacked for concealed quotations; an ever-more intricate filing-system of internal cross-references has been built up; the biblical allusions, Shakespearean correspondences and Wagnerian echoes have been carefully sifted, along with a multitude of lesser debts.

Of all the symbolic schemes in the novel, the Homeric scaffolding is the least controversial. As everyone knows, Joyce partly uses the *Odyssey* to show up the unpoetic and unheroic aspects of modern life; as most readers probably come to recognise, he is equally concerned with the underlying continuities between past and present. The comparison between Bloom and Ulysses is more than a mock-heroic joke, and it cuts both ways, enhancing Bloom's dignity and reminding us that Ulysses, too, had his flesh-and-blood infirmities. In an important sense, as Richard Ellmann says, Bloom *is* Ulysses. But one must add that this identification only holds good at a fairly abstract level, that of common virtues such as prudence, fortitude, faith in the power of reason. As soon as it is translated into more concrete terms, it starts breaking down. Even allowing for cultural differences, for instance, how far can Bloom as a man of the people be equated with a king? And *Ulysses*, unlike *Finnegans Wake*, is a novel where practical distinctions of this kind cannot be disregarded. It is just as well, under the circumstances, that once he has established his major points of comparison Joyce only pursues the Homeric parallels fitfully. They seldom work out very convincingly in detail, and even when they do the effect tends to be blunted by the distracting proximity of other types of symbolism. But the broad correspondences—between Mr Deasy and Nestor, say, or between the newspaper-office and the Palace of the Winds—are for the most part genuinely amusing, and although I don't think one is all that conscious of them from page to page, they do add a larger-than-life comic grandeur when one stands back and views each episode as a whole.

No such claim could be made for most of the other allegorical devices which Stuart Gilbert expounds. It is not so much that Joyce's methods are impermissible as that the ways in which he applies them are so often wholly cerebral, ungainly, mechanical without even having the compensating virtue of machine-like consistency. Few things could be less truly organic, for instance, than the manner in which the organs of the body are strewn across the book; and there must surely come a moment when any but the most slavish Joycean, however willing he may have been to accept Mr Gilbert's guidance at the outset, is finally moved to utter his *non serviam*—'It may be what Joyce intended, but I don't want to know.' (My own decision to defect was prompted by the revelation that in 'The Oxen of the Sun', where the growth of the child in the womb is meant to be symbolised by a series of parodies illustrating the development of English prose, fragments of nineteenth-century scientific jargon are inserted in a paragraph of pastiche-Gibbon in order to indicate the premature development of a part of the embryo.) And what is true in the case of Mr Gilbert applies equally to many of the expositors who have come after him. All too often their labours end up by turning counter-productive, as the ingenuities which they unearth start to seem either pointless or not worth the bother. Take the lines from *Cymbeline* quoted at the very end of 'Scylla and Charybdis', as Stephen emerges from the library into the fresh air:

> Laud we the gods
> And let our crooked smokes climb to their nostrils
> From our bless'd altars.

As a brief coda to the discussion about Shakespeare, suggested by the sight of the smoke curling up from the Dublin chimneypots, this is highly effective; according to one commentator, however—and he is probably right—Joyce was also working in an indirect reference to the episode which immediately follows, 'The Wandering Rocks'. A few lines later in *Cymbeline* someone says 'Let a Roman and a British ensign wave', and the leading public personalities in 'The Wandering Rocks' are Father Conmee (representing the Roman Church) and the Lord

Lieutenant (representing the British Empire). What exactly do we gain by learning this? At best, Joyce could be said to be indulging in a little bookish humour at the expense of literary window-dressing, since even if it were explicitly cited as a chapter-heading the line about the ensigns would seem rather artificially dragged in, like some of the mottoes in George Eliot or Scott. A notable expenditure of effort for the sake of a very small joke— and this is a relatively straightforward specimen of the problems which haunt Joyce scholarship. Anyone familiar with the commentaries on his work could quote far more tortuous examples.

It would be reassuring, at times when the double-meanings and conundrums grow oppressive, to feel that we can simply ignore this whole level of the book if we choose, that, as Hazlitt said of *The Faerie Queene*, if we don't meddle with the allegory, the allegory won't meddle with us. For better or worse, however, a two-tier approach is not really feasible : the allegory has a way of meddling with us even when we try to keep clear of it. A piquant example of this is provided by Anthony Cronin, whose naturalistic, commonsensical account of *Ulysses* is one of the most forceful I know. After soundly drubbing those critics who are so eager to identify Bloom with God the Father or Sinbad the Sailor or Shakespeare or Robinson Crusoe that they forget to think of him as Bloom, Mr Cronin lets slip an original theory of his own : there is a fair case, he argues, bearing in mind Bloom's role as mediator between Stephen and the world of his father, for comparing Bloom to the Holy Ghost. And if this is somewhat inconsistent, it is also an honest acknowledgement of the fact that no intelligent reader of *Ulysses* can altogether avoid being seduced by such analogies, any more than he can turn his back completely on the puzzles or overlook the cross-references. The teasing, enigmatic endlessly suggestive qualities of the book are part of its essential appeal.

Taken piecemeal, the problems are a good deal less daunting than I have so far made them sound. Many of the allusions are perfectly obvious; and even where we have to follow the commentators into obscure corners, the detective-work is often fascinating to watch in itself. (A good example is Marvin Magalaner's tracking-down of the scattered references to the anecdote about the Immaculate Conception—'C'est le pigeon, Joseph'—in his study of Joyce's early fiction, *Time of Apprenticeship*: the trail leads him deep into the strange career of Léo Taxil, who flourished in late nineteenth-century France first as an anti-clerical pornographer and then as a religious charlatan.) Similarly, the recurrent images and minute cross-references, however uncertain we may be about what symbolic meaning if any to attach to them, have a quite independent value from the psychological point of view. Like the interior monologues, they are a stylised literary device rather than an accurate transcription of what normally goes on in the mind, but they do suggest remarkably well the ways in which ideas re-echo, bob up unexpectedly, intermingle, take on the colour of their immediate context.

It is only when we try to weld all the details together, to see the myth of *Ulysses* in its totality, that we run into really serious difficulties. There are dizzying complexities to contend with, and inexplicable contradictions to reconcile; most disconcerting of all, there is the sense of oscillating between the arbitrary and the purposeful, often without any means of deciding which is which. By what scale of values are we to judge whether a detail is structural or decorative, whether an apparently casual allusion is to be given its full weight or not? A few critics would retort that there is an equally good reason for everything in the book. To his out-and-out disciples, Joyce is rather like the girl in the Marie

Lloyd song: 'Every little movement has a meaning of its own, every little motion tells a tale.' But this is not the experience of most readers, and since 1962 the popular verdict has received powerful scholarly confirmation in the shape of Robert Martin Adams' *Surface and Symbol*. By dint of rigorous (and wittily conducted) research, Professor Adams demonstrates as irrefutably as anyone could that 'the meaningless is deeply interwoven with the meaningful in the texture of the novel', that 'the book loses as much as it gains by being read closely', and that 'it is not the product of a pure "aesthetic" impulse'. Joyce's methods were often deliberately haphazard, like those of an artist collecting *objets trouvés*, and in the interests of self-expression he was prepared to make use of the most opaquely autobiographical material.

Once we accept all this, it becomes pointless to keep tunnelling into *Ulysses* in the hope that a central unifying myth will eventually come to light. What we are left with, in my view, is a book which strains after the status of myth, but which can never fully attain it because it is too firmly rooted in the modern secular world. As far as Joyce is concerned, at least, there are no more divinities, and no more epic heroes. (Had he wanted to celebrate the last of the latter he would have written a Parnelliad). At the same time there is just as much heroism in the world as there ever was: it is simply that it tends to manifest itself in fragmentary or unspectacular ways, and that it may take an artist to discern it. Hence we are still surrounded by the broken reflections of past myths, even if we lack a commanding myth of our own. Within his limits, Joyce takes an open-minded view of human nature. 'Who was M'Intosh?' Bloom wonders at the end of his long day, recalling the mysterious stranger in the raincoat at Dignam's funeral. It is one of the most celebrated riddles in the book, and at various times all kinds of answers have been proposed: Christ, Parnell, Mr

Duffy from *Dubliners*, a friend of Joyce's father called Wetherup. But surely the implication is that we can never be certain of what a stranger's potentialities are, or how he is going to turn out. M'Intosh might be anybody.

On the other hand Joyce is not yet ready to say Here Comes Everybody, not even in the case of Bloom. Only at the end of the book, with Molly's soliloquy, does he start moving decisively towards the monomythic universalism of *Finnegans Wake*. Molly is quite explicitly associated by him with Gea-Tellus, the Mother of All Things. She is natural, elemental, eternal; she has a bawdy vitality which encompasses everything else in the book; her thoughts flow on irresistibly, as indifferent to morality as to punctuation, but always heading in the direction of that final 'yes'. If Stephen can only learn to read her aright, she will prove to be his true Muse—the girl on the beach and Rosie O'Grady merged and transformed into an Earth Goddess. Such, at any rate, seems to have been Joyce's intention, and such is the spirit in which she is regularly discussed: Molliolatry is one of the commonest features of Joyce-worship. When we look at the actual substance of her soliloquy, however, she makes a rather different impression. Her jibes are often quite funny, her intimacies have their fascination, and she is shrewd enough to see that Bloom is ultimately a better man than Boylan; but for the most part she comes across as peevish, slatternly and small-minded. Despite the sensual images which tumble through her mind, she mostly lacks warmth; and for an Earth Mother she is not even particularly maternal, either with regard to her own children or to the news about Mrs Purefoy. It is difficult not to feel, in fact, that underneath a show of affection for her Joyce was animated by a good deal of hostility, coupled with a certain amount of abject submissiveness.

Why, then, have so many critics been ready to burn

incense at her shrine? Partly, no doubt, because they find
the idea of an Earth Mother an alluring one in itself;
partly because the rhythm of the book calls out for a
strong positive ending; and partly because in the last two
or three pages (which is what everyone remembers)
Joyce does succeed in working up towards a sunburst of
lyrical affirmation. But the final reverie doesn't automatically transfigure all that has gone before, and it is
hardly eloquent or sustained enough to put Molly in the
same class as, say, the Venus Genetrix of Lucretius,
which is the level at which Joyce is asking to be judged.
Our conclusion must be, I think, that by this stage he
was attempting the impossible, trying to combine the
naturalistic portrayal of a woman with the allegorical
delineation of a goddess. (It would be an impossibility
however sympathetic Molly was at the human level.)
And there is one further lesson to be drawn: whatever
else we may feel about the *Wake*, given that Joyce
conceived of it as a universal myth he made a wise
choice when he decided to override the normal claims of
naturalism completely and cast it in the form of a dream.

5 Blurry Works at Hurdlesford

I

Even as a child Joyce was intensely fascinated by the history and the suggestive power of words, and most of the characters in his books with whom he unmistakably identifies share the same preoccupation. Stephen Hero is equally drawn to academic philology, and to the idea that language possesses occult or semi-magical properties. He pores over Skeat's Etymological Dictionary by the hour; he also studies Blake and Rimbaud on the 'values of letters', after which he tries his hand at shuffling and combining the five vowels in an effort to construct 'cries for primitive emotions'. In the very first paragraph of *Dubliners*, language is shown casting its spell on the youthful narrator. His thoughts dwell obsessively on the word paralysis: 'It had always sounded strangely in my ears, like the word gnomon in the Euclid and the word simony in the Catechism. But now it sounded to me like the name of some maleficent and sinful being.' Stephen Dedalus, too, is mesmerised as a boy by 'queer' words, while as a student he is shown letting his mind drift over the sensuous qualities of language, composing a scrap of nonsense verse about ivy 'whining and twining' and going on to free-associate about yellow ivy, ivory ivy, *ivoire, avorio, ebur*, until the word ivory shines in his brain 'clearer and brighter than any ivory sawn from the mottled tusks of elephants'. (According to Frank Budgen, when Joyce described the texture of a word he sounded like a sculptor talking about a piece of stone.)

The Stephen of the *Portrait* is also troubled by the gap—as he sees it—between English words and Irish feelings. When it comes to a technical term like 'tundish' (the oil-funnel for a lamp) he can give lessons in English to the dean of studies, a true-born Englishman—and yet 'the language in which we are speaking is his before it is mine ... I have not made or accepted its words. My voice holds them at bay.'

Although Joyce's heightened awareness of language supplies some of the subject-matter in his earlier writings, it doesn't lead to any very noteworthy departures in terms of his actual style. Here and there, no doubt, one can faintly discern the promise of future innovations. A fondness for compound adjectives—lightclad, rosefrail—and a prejudice against hyphenating them suggest the first stirrings of an ambition to make words fuse indissolubly together; the bits of dog-Latin bandied about by Stephen and his fellow-students ('Credo ut vos sanguinarius mendax estis', 'Damnum longum tempus prendit') modestly foreshadow the hybrid idioms and polyglot humour of the final phase. But these are mere incidental flourishes. It is only in *Ulysses* that Joyce begins to break down the barriers of conventional usage in earnest, truncating, distorting and splicing together individual words, taking typographical liberties, rearranging word-order, punctuation and syntax for the sake of dramatic emphasis. The novel is both a museum of defunct literary styles and a treasure-house of popular and substandard speech; it also contains examples of every kind of verbal legerdemain or ineptitude, from anagrams to malapropisms, from cryptograms to baby-talk. And in a more pervasive way, Joyce plays the concertina with the average English written sentence, repeatedly favouring either short verbless sentences—'presentative' sentences, as the grammarians say—or lengthy catalogues and proliferating subordinate clauses. Molly's nocturnal soliloquy simply carries the latter tendency to its logical conclusion.

The linguistic exuberance of *Ulysses* is part of the book's general vitality, and taken separately most of Joyce's unorthodox procedures can be seen to serve a definite novelistic purpose. They are meant to express particular states of consciousness, to render a scene more vividly, to provide sardonic comments on the action. But there are so many of them, and they are sown so thickly in the text, that the style increasingly draws attention to itself as the book progresses. Language in *Ulysses* is not a transparent medium; we are made too aware of its quirks, and of the ways in which it lends itself to manipulation. To take one small aspect of a very large topic, consider some of the uses which Joyce makes of initials and capital letters. Stephen thinks ruefully of the books he once planned to write with letters for titles. ('Have you read his F? O yes, but I prefer Q. Yes, but W is wonderful. O yes, W.') The five H.E.L.Y.'S sandwich-men parade around the city with the H pushing ahead and the Y lagging behind. Bloom takes the handout from the Y.M.C.A. young man, sees the poet A.E. and wonders what the A and the E stand for, tries to recollect the popular explanation of the sacred initials I.N.R.I. ('Iron nails ran in'). Poor Breen is driven frantic by an anonymous postcard bearing the terse message 'U.P.' Stephen, in the library, ponders on the mystery of how individual identity persists while the personality changes ('I, I and I. I.'), suddenly remembers that he still owes A.E. some money ('A.E.I.O.U.'), and speculates tipsily about Shakespeare's Mr W.H. ('Mr William Himself'). Father Conmee S.J. stops for a chat with the wife of Mr David Sheehy M.P., and strolls past a shut-up free church with a notice announcing that 'the reverend T. R. Green B.A. will (D.V.) speak'. Bloom writes I AM A in the sand, which as William York Tindall points out could mean anything or everything—either 'I am a?' (message incomplete) or 'I am Alpha' (and Omega). F.A.B.P. was part of the code used by the great Ignatius Gallaher when he cabled his legendary scoop about the Phoenix Park murders to New York; 'K.M.R.I.A.' means 'Kiss my royal Irish arse'. The clandestine flirtation which Bloom, alias Henry Flower, has been conducting by post with the unknown Martha Clifford is reduced to a problem in a mathematics textbook: he adds to the collection of oddments which he keeps locked up in his writing-table 'a letter received by Henry Flower (let H.F. be L.B.) from Martha Clifford (find M.C.)'. Stephen and Bloom exchange cultural confidences by embellishing a copy of *The Sweets of Sin* with half a dozen characters written in Irish and Hebrew script respectively ... And the list of such items could easily be extended over several pages. True, not all of them are particularly striking in themselves; but their cumulative effect is to sharpen our sense of the alphabet as a limited yet inexhaustible set of symbols, to underline how variable and at the same time how extraordinarily potent are the values we assign to individual letters. Even a missing letter, in an atmosphere as charged as this, acquires far more significance than it would in a less strenuously self-conscious linguistic context. A newspaper misprint transforms Bloom into 'L. Boom', and for an instant he becomes a man of no account, his identity blotted out by a hollow reverberation from the Palace of Aeolus.[1]

1. It is ironical that the reporter at Dignam's funeral had made a special point of getting Bloom's Christian name right, and there are further alphabetical ironies, as anyone who looks up the relevant passage in 'Eumaeus' will see, in the inclusion of Stephen and M'Intosh in the list of mourners. Joyce is seldom content to make only one point at a time with his wordplay. The day-dream about ivory in the *Portrait*, for instance, which at first sight looks like an exercise in pure aestheticism, carries concealed religious and sexual connotations; it refers back (although Stephen him-

In *Ulysses* language is already beginning to work loose from its hinges; in *Finnegans Wake* it breaks free completely, and words take on a capricious life of their own. Artefacts rather than labels, whirling centres of energy rather than static clear-cut units, they coalesce, subdivide and exert a magnetic attraction over one another in terms of their formal affinities. The result is a non-stop verbal pantomime, a marathon charade, an unparalleled 'guessmasque'. All kinds of partial precedents can be cited, from the macaronic verse of the later Middle Ages to the more hermetic experiments of the French *symbolistes*; Joyce himself pays his respects to the 'little language' of Swift's *Journal to Stella* and to Lewis Carroll (whom oddly enough he has never read until the first extracts from *Work in Progress* were published, and people began pointing out the resemblance between his coinages and the portmanteau-words of Jabberwocky). But none of his precursors, as far as I know, manage to sustain anything like the same degree of complexity, certainly not at such formidable length. To say that the principal stylistic device employed in the *Wake* is the pun, for instance, is to give a very pale and inadequate idea of the full-blown possibilities of Joycean wordplay. By the internal standards of the book, pure puns, in the sense of double meanings which turn on exact homonyms, are in fact not all that common—i.e. there are probably not more than a dozen or so per page. Far more frequent are the near-puns which are hinted at by means of orthographical nuances and slight structural distortions, the phantom puns conjured up by the pressure of an idiom, a familiar cadence, a leit-motif, the compound verbal fractures which send splinters of mean-

---

self seems unaware of it) to childhood memories of the effeminate Tusker Boyle, and of comparing a girl to a Tower of Ivory, a phrase from the Litany for the Virgin 'which protestants could not understand'.

ing flying off in five or six different directions at once. All the linguistic resources exhibited in *Ulysses*, from onomatopoeia to alphabet symbolism, are brought into play, but far more intricately and intensively than in the earlier book, with far fewer concessions to ordinary usage; there are also rich accretions from the various languages which Joyce knew, and light sprinklings of vocabulary from many of those which he didn't. Finally, the syntax of the *Wake* is every bit as unstable as the diction. Sentences change course unaccountably, stop short, slither out of the reader's grasp. We negotiate our way round an unwieldy parenthesis, only to be immediately confronted by another; we get an imperative where we expect a negative, an adverb where we expect a preposition. And while all this is going on Joyce steadfastly maintains the tone of a man who is either making perfect sense already, or doing his best to clear up any obscure points which may still be troubling us. From a distance his exclamations, footnotes, rhetorical questions and judicious asides create the illusion of a coherent argument, and suggest that he is whole-heartedly taking us into his confidence; it is only on closer inspection that the façade of logic dissolves, and we find ourselves floundering among the booby-traps and false perspectives.

Wake-talk is anything but empty gibberish, however. On the contrary, what we have to contend with while trying to decipher it is an unmanageable excess of meaning—or rather, of secondary meanings, minor associations and allusions which continually send the reader off at a tangent. (One effect of the trick syntax, incidentally, is to encourage us to pause at every comma, and linger even longer than we might otherwise have done over the polysemantic implications of individual words and phrases.) It is true that with a little practice we can often make out the underlying drift of a passage, and that the book as a whole would be very much less baffling if we were able to apply a kind of Occam's razor to the ambiguities and concentrate exclusively on one hard core of meaning in every case. But it is in the nature of the *Wake* to resist simplification, and to keep tantalising the reader with will-o'-the-wisp alternative renderings and side-turnings which may or may not lead somewhere important—with questions of shemantics, as one might say.

What was Joyce's object in devising so outlandish a style?—always assuming, that is, that the entire book isn't best regarded as a hoax. The earliest commentators on the *Wake*, frequently taking their cue from various remarks which Joyce himself made about his nocturnal aesthetic and about 'putting the language to sleep', tended to assume that he was trying to imitate the actual language of dreams, and undoubtedly it is all too easy to rifle the book for examples of dreamlike displacement and condensation, for the involuntary verbal tremors which betray suppressed guilt or anxiety. When insects make their appearance, thoughts of incest are seldom very far behind, and when the inner censor nods an innocent-sounding fairy-tale is always liable to turn into the old story of 'a little rude hiding rod'. But these are small-scale effects; nobody ever dreamed in Joycean puns for six hundred pages at a time, and viewed as a whole the dream-language of the *Wake*, like the dream itself, is a highly artificial literary convention, altogether lacking the starkness and clarity of the real thing. If Joyce nevertheless seems to be illustrating Freud's dictum that words, as the nodal points of numerous ideas, are inherently ambiguous, it is primarily for metaphysical rather than psychological reasons. In the *Wake* everything flows, and everything returns to its source; there is limitless diversity, and underlying unity; personal identity is an epiphenomenon, and past, present, and future are rolled up together. To embody this vision, the pun (together with all its variants) makes the perfect vehicle. As the temporary point of intersection at which normally disparate forces coincide, it represents both fission and fusion, both stasis and flux. Ideally, no doubt, Joyce would have liked to have been able to fashion a supreme all-embracing cosmic pun, a One subsuming the Many; failing that, he set out to create a sort of literary perpetual-motion machine, a contrivance designed to throw up fresh puzzles and reveal hidden relationships *ad infinitum*. If he couldn't solve the riddle of the universe, at least he was determined to propound it more exhaustively than any previous writer. And whatever one may think of such an ambition, one must, I think, agree that it supplies a driving force which radically distinguishes his incessant wordplay from that of his imitators. Without some such rationale, attempts to pun on the Joycean scale are doomed to be mere mechanical exercises—as Edmund Burke said of a contemporary who tried to model his style on Dr Johnson, 'the contortions of the Sibyl without the inspiration'.

At the same time I don't myself believe that every single word in the *Wake* can be accounted for 'philosophically', still less that this is the only profitable way of looking at the language of the book. There are many other valid if less central avenues of approach, ranging from the philological to the cabbalistic. One can still discern very clearly in Joyce—some would say on every page—the youthful reader of Rimbaud and Blake, with his half-belief in spells and incantations, in the possibility of bringing to light a secret *alchimie du verbe*. One can also recognise the erstwhile devotee of Skeat, although his interest in etymology has been incomparably broadened by his reading of Vico, who saw no essential difference between the study of language and the study of history, and who argued that words encapsulate the past experience of the race. (Naturally Joyce jollies this theory along with innumerable false derivations, so that Adam's apple-tree becomes an 'upfellbowm' and a cloak of civilised decency is thrown over primitive cloacal activities.) Nor do the sophistication and the arcane aspects of the language of the *Wake* preclude a great deal of deliberate childishness on Joyce's part. His methods enable him to regress to the stage of playful experimentation which marks our first secure mastery of speech, to recapture something of the child's pleasure in fondling and fooling around with the words which he has just learned or (since play can be destructive too) in tearing them to pieces.

Finally, it is important to bear in mind that for all its eccentricities the basic language of the *Wake* is English, and spoken English at that. The vitality of the book derives primarily from its colloquial flavour, from the intonations of Irish talk, from the humour which Joyce was able to extract from conversational clichés (often by giving the words their maximum value) and the delight which he took in such linguistic odds and ends as music-hall crosstalk, heraldic mottoes, schoolboy tags. There is an account by Padraic Colum, for instance, of Joyce at a dinner-party in Paris, quoting one of the mnemonic rhymes from a Latin grammar—

> *With* nemo *never let me see*
> Neminis *or* Nemine

and doubling up with laughter: 'Oh, the imperiousness of it! "Never let me see!" ' To my mind an anecdote like that reveals more of the spirit which animates the *Wake*—in its more successful aspects, at least—than many a solemn discussion of Joyce's theoretical intentions. In the abstract the book can easily be made to sound fearsomely pedantic, a grammarian's funeral; in practice it is a prodigious feast of language, and if it were nothing else it would always be worth dipping into for the sake of its seductive verbal beauties and ingenuities. But to consider it solely in such terms is also, of course, to settle for incidental rewards, to write off the controlling scheme as stillborn and much of the detail as hopelessly arid. However great its curiosity-value, as a work of art on the scale which Joyce intended the *Wake* stands or falls by its central myth, and it is to the assumptions underlying that myth that we must now turn.

II

An elementary problem looms up at the outset: we are dealing with a book which is largely incomprehensible at a first reading, and not much clearer at a second—unless, that is, we are prepared to cling to the experts from the very beginning, and to lean far more heavily on their guidance than a self-respecting reader would normally consent to do in the case of almost any other novelist or poet. Even then, our difficulties are hardly at an end, since specialist opinion is often sharply divided, often on the most fundamental points. As crucial a question as the identity of the Dreamer still remains unresolved, for instance. In the words of Ruth von Phul, 'Who sleeps at *Finnegans Wake*?' Is it H. C. Earwicker, or Shem, or James Joyce, or Finn MacCool, or an omniscient narrator, or a whole succession of dreamers, so that (to quote Mitchell Morse) 'the narrator is always somebody who could be the narrator of the particular passage in question'? Perhaps no final answer is possible, or even necessary; but before we can judge that, we must become more expert than the experts. Equally, there are striking discrepancies between the various synopses of the 'plot' which commentators have attempted—and who shall decide, when Mrs Glasheen, Professor Tindall, Professor Benstock, and Messrs Campbell and Robinson disagree? This is not to malign the 'Joyce industry', which has often been very unfairly ridiculed.[2] Some extremely acute and amazingly tenacious scholarship has gone into unravelling the *Wake*, and as a member of the laity I am duly grateful. My quarrel is not with the exegetes, but with those features of the book which make exegesis on such a scale essential. When Joyce said that he expected his readers to devote their entire lives to his work, or when he invoked an ideal reader 'suffering from an ideal insomnia', I don't think he was altogether joking; and the ambition seems to me infantile, that of the small child who demands his parents' undivided attention, and who is determined to keep them staying up all night with him if he possibly can.

It is true that certain other authors have been studied just as intensively, and Joyce was well aware of them as rival attractions, especially 'great Shapesphere'. But there is one vital difference. However much the commentaries on *King Lear* may enhance or deepen our understanding, we don't need them in order to see what the play is all about. The closest precedents for *Wake*-scholarship, in fact, are to be found outside secular literature, in the devout expositions of those sacred books which the faithful are ready to explore indefinitely, since they believe that every syllable which they contain is divinely inspired. Even the scriptural analogy is very imperfect—one doesn't have to be a Talmudist to understand the Ten Commandments—but it will serve; and the question which then arises is in what sense the *Wake* can be said

2. It has its lunatic fringe, of course: a writer as eccentric as Joyce is bound to bring out eccentricity in others, and to attract more than his fair share of cranks. Not for nothing is the paranoid professor in Mary McCarthy's *The Groves of Academe* a Joyce man, for instance.

to deserve the same minute attention. It isn't, one need hardly add, a matter of whether or not Joyce's mythology is literally true, but of how illuminating we find it as a poetic metaphor, and how far it tallies with the deepest facts of our experience.

The two most fundamental axioms of the *Wake* are that history endlessly repeats itself, and that the part always implies the whole. Civilisations rise and fall according to a preordained cyclic pattern, and as the wheel turns the same characters, events, and institutions come round again under different guises. As for personal identity, it is only skin-deep, a temporal and temporary variation (dial TIM for Finnegan) on an eternal theme. The self, far from being unique, is a microcosm, one of innumerable similarly-constructed 'celves'; hence, incidentally, Joyce's fondness for apophony and the ablaut, for shifting vowels encased in the same hard shell of consonants ('Fiatfuit', 'impovernment of the booble by the bauble for the bubble'). On this particular occasion, the potentialities of the species happen to be summed up in Earwicker, but then, as Molly said of Bloom, 'as well him as another'. By virtue of being the head of a family, he is all patriarchs; by virtue of having aggressive instincts, he is all warriors; by virtue of being a man, he is all men. And if these ubiquitous qualities deprive him of absolute individuality, they confer immortality on him in return. In the Joycean scheme of things, parallels overlap, and repetition ensures regeneration. Finnegan may be dead, but the common human nature of which he partakes won't lie down; and in one of the neatest of the formulas which echo through the book, birthday greetings are incessantly offered and universally reciprocated : 'Teems of times and happy returns. The seim anew.' Or in other words, the mixture as before—and the same to you.

In the modern world we are so thoroughly habituated

to the idea of time as a kind of irreversible conveyor-belt that most of us are likely to recoil from a cyclic theory of history as a piece of self-evident nonsense. But at least Joyce can fairly claim that he has the authority of the past on his side. The myth of the Eternal Return, to borrow the title of Mircea Eliade's magisterial survey, is among the most ancient and widespread of supernatural beliefs. Very few civilisations apart from our own have had an essentially linear conception of time, and even in the West, although Christianity broke the circuit by insisting on the historical uniqueness of the Crucifixion, it was not until the scientific revolution of the seventeenth century that the linear view finally prevailed. For earlier societies, it was the principle of eternal recurrence, of the regeneration of time, which more than any other guaranteed universal stability, and which enabled men to fend off what Eliade calls *la terreur de l'histoire*—that same 'nightmare of history' which the Stephen Dedalus of *Ulysses* is trying to escape.

As heresies go, then, the cyclic myth has a respectable pedigree. It answers a deep human craving, and it has at least some basis in biological experience, in the cycle of the generations. Moreover, for primitive man life actually was exceedingly repetitive. He was confined to his own culture, his whole existence was bound up with the rhythm of the seasons, the structure of his society admitted of very few individual variations. Still, none of this makes living in the modern era any less of a complex fate. We know too much; the old escape-routes from history have been sealed off, and it has become progressively harder for an educated writer to maintain a world-view as archaic and compact as Joyce's without either rigging the evidence or retreating into shadowy generalities.

On the face of it he tries to confront the issues squarely. The *Wake* brims over with what look like historical data : it is packed with allusions to the most heterogeneous periods and places, and hundreds of famous names from the history-books figure among the cast of supporting players. But the over-all effect is garish, anecdotal and absurd, and bears about as much relation to the history written about by genuine historians as would an afternoon spent going round Madame Tussaud's. This is precisely what Joyce intends (and one should add that he is never more entertaining than when he is guying just such a tuppence-coloured view of the past—in the brilliantly funny tour of the Willingdone Museyroom, for instance). Throughout the book History is treated as a chaotic mixture of legend, hearsay, gossip, innuendo, apologia, boastful supposition, garbled fact. Rival interpreters display completely contradictory portrayals of the same event in our 'notional gullery'; the decrepit analists mumble on about their 'Blubby wares upat Ublanium', 'Blurry works at Hurdlesford', 'Bloody wars in Ballyaughacleeaghbally', 'Blotty words for Dublin'—they can't even seem to get the name right. (Dublin is Eblana in Latin and Baile Atha Cliath, the city of the ford of hurdles, in Irish.)

As a serio-comic running commentary on our inability to master the past all this is acceptable, if overdone, and as a burlesque version of the ways in which malice and *folie de grandeur* have coloured historical attitudes, it is often extremely amusing—when it isn't alarming. But what of the actual events which men live through, as opposed to the constructions and misconstructions which they put on them afterwards? In order to uphold his system, Joyce is compelled to devalue history as well as historiography, to drain individual episodes of any specific once-and-for-all significance. He does this chiefly by flattening out and neutralising the element of conflict in human affairs. All wars and combats in the *Wake* are part of the same basic quarrel, which means that they are kept in the family, and all antagonists (of the same sex, at least) are ultimately interchangeable, which means that they are fighting with rubber daggers. We can't even be sure that Shem and Shaun, the eternal opposites, were not swapped round by mistake in infancy.

Having drawn the sting from historical conflict, Joyce also conjures away the problem of evil. Earwicker, the 'fafafather of all schemes for to bother us', carries mankind's guilt on his shoulders; the corollary, as Bernard Benstock points out, is that he has committed all sins. But they are sins rather than crimes, and the sense of guilt which attaches to them is directly derived from the sexual fantasies and misapprehensions of early childhood. Whatever the exact nature of the original offence committed in Phoenix Park, the main elements involved seem to have been spying, self-exposure, making homosexual advances, watching girls urinate; and while Earwicker's guilty stammer betrays a bad conscience over his encounter with the Cad, it also suggests that the whole affair may have been nothing worse than the story of a 'caca Cad'. In the same way, 'the first riddle of the universe' which the infant Shem puts to his brothers and sisters—'when is a man not a man?'—receives many different answers in the course of the book (including, by implication, 'when she's a woman'), but never, I think, 'when he's inhuman'. Detesting brutality and physical violence in real life, Joyce transforms them into buffoonery, and his Everyman emerges as an old sinner only in the indulgent, half-jocular meaning of the phrase: he is Human, Erring, Condonable. A splendid knockabout reprobate, in whom we all ought to be able to recognise some of our weaknesses and vanities—but like Bloom, too amiable and too peripheral to represent the forces which wield control in society at large.

It is at the level of his instinctual urges and conflicts

that his deepest claim to universality lies. Disdainful of psychoanalysis, Joyce certainly did not set out with any intention of laying bare Earwicker's unconscious; but by devising a literary form which gave exceptionally free play to his fantasies he succeeded, almost in spite of himself, in creating a picture of psychological man—and psychological man, in Freudian terms at least, is universal man. To quote a representative view, that of Franz Alexander, 'in the deep unconscious all men are akin; individuality is formed nearer the surface'.

However, the argument of the *Wake* is History, not Psychology, and by reducing social life to its earliest familial constituents Joyce falls into perpetrating his own home-made brand of psychologism. Important though it may be for us to search out the universal aspects of human nature, we normally face our problems and make our choices in a world where to be a millionaire is *not* the same thing as to be a landless peasant, where to paint like Rembrandt is *not* the same thing as designing chocolate-boxes, and where a Hitler, if he was once a helpless baby, also grew up to be—Hitler. No doubt there is a certain fundamental pathos in the thought that our greatest achievements and ugliest faults have their origins in childhood: Kipling captures it very well in his poem 'A St Helena Lullaby', where at one level Napoleon never leaves the playroom—'And after all your trapesings, child, lie still!' But Kipling also has a much stronger sense than Joyce of the public career, of history as

> the undoctored incident
> That actually occurred.

By contrast, Napoleon in the *Wake* remains 'Lipoleum', the small boy who identifies with his mother and who is afraid that he will be ridden over roughshod by his father, the Iron Duke sitting on his 'big wide harse'. Given that Joyce is describing a dream, he is entitled to concern himself as exclusively as this with mankind's fantasy-life; but given that he has also taken the whole of history for his province, there is something frivolous and slightly indecent about his attitude. In our waking hours, after all, fantasies get acted out, and ideas have consequences.

Some Joyceans, I know, would say that this is making heavy weather of a work which is essentially comic in conception. Joyce himself protested that his aim was to make readers laugh, and on occasion the *Wake* has even been approvingly described *tout court* as a farce. That it frequently deals with slapstick situations, and that it brings off a constant succession of unashamed gags, few would deny. But personally I have too much respect for Joyce to believe that he devoted nearly twenty years of his life to producing nothing more considerable than a kind of mammoth highbrow version of *1066 and All That*; and, more to the point, for all its sunny levity the book is often clouded over with darker emotions— anxiety, disgust, resentment, self-pity, remorse. If, in spite of this, the hint of farce keeps returning, it is because the one thing which by definition Joyce can't achieve in the *Wake* is tragic finality. 'Booms of bombs and heavy rethudders? This aim to you!' But since we are going to rise from our ashes like the Phoenix, it isn't a threat we can altogether take seriously.

In the end the *Wake* seems to me a dazzling failure, the aberration of a great man. Viewed as a whole, I don't believe it is nearly worth the effort which it demands; but it would be a pity if potential readers were frightened off by the all-or-nothing Joyce fanatics, when there is so much pleasure to be obtained even from random dipping or concentrating on a few favourite passages. Half the fascination, in fact, lies in the incidentals, in spotting the jokes and following up the references. Expecting an apocalyptic revelation, we are repeatedly brought down to earth—to this or that specific patch of earth; and we can never be sure whose features besides Earwicker's are going to peep out next from behind the blank mask of Everyman. How satisfying to discover, for instance, that HCE stands for 'Haveth Childers Everywhere' partly because there was a minor Victorian statesman called Hugh Culling Eardley Childers, whose parliamentary nickname was 'Here Comes Everybody'. As well him as another; but anyone who has come under the spell of the *Wake* will be glad to learn of his unique ineluctable existence. For despite Joyce's universalising ambitions, his greatest strength as a writer is that he rejoices in the 'plurability' of life, in the endlessly unpredictable shapes which it assumes. And despite his teems of times and his cyclic patterns, what he finally laments, in Anna Livia's superb dying monologue, is life's transience—or so I would judge. Ostensibly Anna Livia is under 'a suspended sentence': if we keep reading we will find that we are circling back to the beginning, and that life is about to begin all over again. But the resurrection-machinery looks creaky and unconvincing by comparison with the swansong itself, and nothing else in the book has the power of the last overwhelming premonitions of death: the 'therrble prongs'; the despairing cry of 'mememormee!' ('remember me', with mortality at the heart of it); the child at last reconciled with the father—'Carry me along, taddy, like you done through the toy fair!' (According to Richard Ellman, this is an echo of Joyce carrying his son George through a toy fair in Trieste to make up for not giving him a rocking horse.) And that concluding 'the': perhaps for the one and only time in the course of writing the *Wake* Joyce's feeling for words failed him when he told Louis Gillet that he had decided to end with it because it was 'the least accented, the weakest word in English, a word which is not even a word, which is scarcely sounded between the teeth, a breath, a nothing'. In fact it can be an exceptionally difficult word to pronounce, as countless foreigners know—and its implications are immense. It is the definite article: it speaks for a world where everything has its own identity and where you only live once, for the finality which the rest of the book strains to deny.

H. C. E. CHILDERS.

H(ERE) C(OMES) E(VERYBODY)
CH-LD-RS.''

From 'M.P.'s in Session', by Harry Furniss, published by Bradbury, Agnew

Bibliographical Note

The dates are those of the first English edition except where indicated.

Books by Joyce

Stephen Hero (first pub. 1944)
Chamber Music (1907)
Dubliners (1914)
A Portrait of the Artist as a Young Man (New York, 1916; London, 1917)
Ulysses (Paris, 1922; London, 1937)
Pomes Penyeach (Paris, 1927; London, 1932)
Finnegans Wake (1939)
The Critical Writings of James Joyce, ed. Ellsworth Mason and Richard Ellmann (1959)
Giacomo Joyce, ed. Richard Ellmann (1968)
Letters of James Joyce, vol. I ed. Stuart Gilbert (1957), vols. II & III ed. Richard Ellmann (1966)
Selected Letters of James Joyce, ed. Richard Ellmann (1976).

Further Reading

The Joyce literature is vast, and growing vaster; it would take a book much longer than the present one to list all the items. What follows is simply meant to light the way a little for the general reader. Most of the books I have included are readily available, and many of them contain substantial bibliographies.

a) Biographical

The standard biography is Richard Ellmann's *James Joyce* (1959). A useful resumé, with some excellent illustrations, can be found in Chester G. Anderson, *James Joyce and his World* (1967). Frank Budgen, *James Joyce and the Making of Ulysses* (1934; reissued 1960) and Stanislaus Joyce, *My Brother's Keeper* (1959) are both works of exceptional literary merit in their own right. J. B. Lyons, *James Joyce and Medicine* (1973) offers a doctor's account of the medical facts, both of Joyce and his family's illnesses, and of Joyce's fiction. See also:

Sylvia Beach, *Shakespeare and Company* (1960)
Frank Budgen, *My Selves When Young* (1970)
Mary and Padraic Colum, *Our Friend James Joyce* (1958)
Stan Gébler Davies, *James Joyce: A Portrait of the Artist* (1975)
Louis Gillet, *Claybook for James Joyce* (Paris, 1946; English translation, 1958)
Ulick O'Connor, *Oliver St John Gogarty* (1963)
Kevin Sullivan, *Joyce among the Jesuits* (1958). On Joyce's education.

b) General

Harry Levin's *James Joyce* (1944; revised ed. 1960) is probably still the best general introduction. Other compact introductory surveys include:

Anthony Burgess, *Here Comes Everybody* (1965)
Anthony Burgess, *Joysprick: An Introduction to the Language of James Joyce* (1973)
S. L. Goldberg, *Joyce* (1962)
Kenneth Grose, *James Joyce* (1975)
A. Walton Litz, *James Joyce* (New York, 1966)
William York Tindall, *James Joyce, His Way of Interpreting the Modern World* (1950)

Longer studies include:
Hugh Kenner, *Dublin's Joyce* (1955). Exasperating but highly stimulating.
Marvin Magalaner and Richard Kain, *Joyce: The Man, the Work, the Reputation* (1956)
J. Mitchell Morse, *The Sympathetic Alien* (1959). Joyce and Catholicism.
William York Tindall, *A Reader's Guide to James Joyce* (1959)
Seon Givens, *James Joyce: Two Decades of Criticism* (New York, 1948) is a valuable anthology. A comprehensive selection of critical comment on Joyce up to 1941 can be found in the two volumes of *James Joyce: The Critical Heritage*, ed. Robert Deming (1970). Ezra Pound's letters to Joyce and essays on his work have been collected in *Pound/Joyce: Letters and Essays*, ed. Forrest Read (1967)

Joyce

Among the many works which contain chapters or sections on Joyce are:

Cyril Connolly, *The Condemned Playground* (1945)

David Daiches, *The Novel and the Modern World* (1939; revised ed. 1960)

Frederick Hoffman, *Freudianism and the Literary Mind* (Baton Rouge, 1945)

Herbert Howarth, *The Irish Writers 1880-1940* (1958)

Hugh Kenner, *The Stoic Comedians* (1962)

Wyndham Lewis, *Time and Western Man* (1927)

Vivian Mercier, *The Irish Comic Tradition* (1962)

J. I. M. Stewart, *Eight Modern Writers* (1963)

Edmund Wilson, *Axel's Castle* (1931). The best single starting-point.

Two uncollected articles of particular interest are:

F. R. Leavis, 'James Joyce and "The Revolution of the Word"' in *Scrutiny*, II (1933)

Lionel Trilling, 'James Joyce in his Letters', *Commentary*, (February 1968)

c) Individual Works

On the earlier books:

Marvin Magalaner, *Time of Apprenticeship* (1959)

James Joyce's Dubliners: Critical Essays ed. Clive Hart (1969)

Joyce's 'Portrait': Criticisms and Critiques ed. Thomas Connolly (New York, 1962)

On *Ulysses*:

Robert Martin Adams, *Surface and Symbol* (New York, 1962)

Stuart Gilbert, *James Joyce's Ulysses* (1930; revised ed. 1952)

S. L. Goldberg, *The Classical Temper* (1961). The outstanding full-length study.

Richard Ellmann, *Ulysses on the Liffey* (1972)

Richard Kain, *Fabulous Voyager* (Chicago, 1947)

William Schutte, *Joyce and Shakespeare* (New Haven, 1957)

Clive Hart and David Hayman, eds. *James Joyce's Ulysses: Critical Essays* (1974)

Clive Hart and Leo Knuth, *A Topographical Guide to James Joyce's Ulysses* (University of Essex, 1975)

See also W. B. Stanford, *The Ulysses Theme* (1954) for the metamorphoses of Odysseus in Western literature.

Among uncollected articles, it is worth looking up:
R. P. Blackmur, 'The Jew in Search of a Son', *Virginia Quarterly Review*, 1948
William Empson, 'The Theme of *Ulysses*', *Kenyon Review*, 1956

On *Finnegans Wake:*
J. S. Atherton, *The Books at the Wake* (1959; revised ed. New York, 1974). Particularly fascinating.
Bernard Benstock, *Joyce-Again's Wake* (1965)
Joseph Campbell and Henry Morton Robinson, *A Skeleton Key to Finnegans Wake* (New York, 1944; London, 1947). A heroic pioneering effort, but not to be relied on uncritically.
Jack Dalton and Clive Hart, eds. *Twelve and a Tilly*, essays on the 25th anniversary of *Finnegans Wake* (1966)
Adaline Glasheen, *A Second Census of Finnegans Wake* (Northwestern University, 1963). Indispensable.
Clive Hart, *Structure and Motif in Finnegans Wake* (1962). The most penetrating study of the over-all design.
Matthew Hodgart and Mabel Worthington, *Song in the Works of James Joyce* (New York, 1959)
A. Walton Litz, *The Art of James Joyce* (1961)
William York Tindall, *A Reader's Guide to Finnegans Wake* (1969)
Michael H. Begnall and Fritz Senn, *A Conceptual Guide to Finnegans Wake* (1974)
Edmund Wilson, 'The Dream of H. C. Earwicker' in *The Wound and the Bow* (1947)
Anthony Burgess has edited *A Shorter Finnegans Wake* (1966)

Fontana Paperbacks Non-fiction

Fontana is a leading paperback publisher of non-fiction, both popular and academic. Below are some recent titles.

- [ ] AN AUTOBIOGRAPHY   Peter Alliss £1·95
- [ ] BOB HOPE: PORTRAIT OF A SUPERSTAR   Charles Thompson £1·75
- [ ] SUBJECT WOMEN   Ann Oakley £2·75
- [ ] HOW TO GET RID OF THE BOMB   Gavin Scott £1·95
- [ ] POLICEMAN'S PATCH   Harry Cole £1·50
- [ ] A YEAR IN THE DRINK   Martin Green £1·75
- [ ] SCOTLAND   introduction by Lord Home £4·95
- [ ] THE NO-DIET BOOK   Michael Spira £1·50
- [ ] SIR JAMES GOLDSMITH   Geoffrey Wansell £1·95
- [ ] THE CINDERELLA COMPLEX   Colette Dowling £1·75
- [ ] DIANA, THE PRINCESS OF WALES   Hugh Montgomery-Massingberd £1·95
- [ ] SONIA ALLISON'S FOOD PROCESSOR COOKBOOK   £1·95
- [ ] THE ENTERTAINING COOKBOOK   Evelyn Rose £3·95
- [ ] WAR AND SOCIETY IN REVOLUTIONARY EUROPE 1770–1870   Geoffrey Best £2·95
- [ ] EUROPEAN EMPIRES FROM CONQUEST TO COLLAPSE 1815–1960   Victor Kiernan £2·95
- [x] DARWIN   Wilma George £1·75
- [ ] THIS IS WINDSURFING   Reinhart Winkler £5·95
- [ ] CHAMPION'S STORY   Bob Champion & Jonathan Powell £1·50

You can buy Fontana paperbacks at your local bookshop or newsagent. Or you can order them from Fontana Paperbacks, Cash Sales Department, Box 29, Douglas, Isle of Man. Please send a cheque, postal or money order (not currency) worth the purchase price plus 10p per book (or plus 12p per book if outside the UK).

NAME (Block letters)
_____

ADDRESS
_____

_____

_____